MW00907618

A PASSIONATE COOK

MARGARET FULTON

A PASSIONATE COOK

FOOD STYLING BY SUZANNE GIBBS
PHOTOGRAPHS BY RODNEY WEIDLAND

LANSDOWNE

ACKNOWLEDGEMENTS

What gives me enormous happiness is to see the love of food and passion
for cooking passed on from my mother and through me to my daughter Suzanne
Gibbs. I spend many fulfilling hours with Suzanne in the kitchen, planning a meal for
six or a party for six or twenty, discussing the best way to cook a whole salmon or a
good loaf of bread, or fresh fish. All this has kept us the best of friends, bonded by our
shared commitment to fine cooking. It is natural that Suzanne has worked with me
on this book—when two enthusiastic cooks get together it's joy all around.
A very special word of appreciation for a very special photographer,
Rodney Weidland, who is able to bring the food prepared in my kitchen to life.
Amber Keller is an important member of our team who, through years of application,
has become a dedicated and skilled cook. Barbara Beckett is the key to this book.
Her faith in me and my passion for food resulted in this book being
published and its final look.
Nutrition is an essential science and my involvement as an Honorary
Governor of the University of Sydney Nutrition Research Foundation keeps
me up to date with the latest research. I appreciate the contribution nutritionists
make towards a better understanding of food. Organisations such as Oldways, an
international body which brought to world attention the Mediterranean diet,
remind us of the legitimacy of the old ways found in traditional cuisines. The
International Olive Oil Council has also helped educate food writers and
gives them a better knowledge of how other peoples eat. The understanding
of the role of food in our welfare is the better for such bodies.

MARGARET FULTON

PUBLISHED BY LANSDOWNE PUBLISHING PTY LTD

Level 1, 18 Argyle Street, Sydney NSW 2000, Australia

First published 1998

© Copyright text 1998: Margaret Fulton
© Copyright design 1998: Lansdowne Publishing Pty Ltd

Design: Barbara Beckett
Copy Editor: Siobhan O'Connor
Set in Garamond, Trajan and Copperplate on Quark Xpress
Printed in Hong Kong

National Library of Australia Cataloguing-in-Publication data
Fulton, Margaret.
A passionate cook.
Includes index.
ISBN 1 86302 621 5.
1 Cookery. 1 Title.
641.5

Produced in association with Barbara Beckett Publishing Pty Ltd
14 Hargrave Street, Paddington, Sydney, Australia 2021

PHOTOGRAPHS: Quail with Grapes (page 2); Garden Salad with Roasted Goat's
Cheese Croûtes (page 3); Salade Maison (page 6)

CONTENTS

INTRODUCTION

MY PASSION for cooking was fuelled, first and foremost, by the sheer joy of eating all the sublime things that came out of my mother's kitchen. A perfectly roasted chicken, a plump young bird, butter roasted with its crisp golden skin and meltingly tender flesh was a feast for the eyes and perhaps best of all a feast for the soul. It would invariably have a delicious stuffing and be accompanied by young vegetables from a home garden, a mushroom gravy if we had been out in the fields and discovered a magical fairy mushroom ring.

TRADITIONS die hard and today we are witnessing a revival of old ways, including those seemingly effortless but wonderful roast dinners mother used to make. Did she have special tricks up her sleeve that turned this simple meal into a monument to good living and memories? There is a revival, too, of those superb dishes that emerged from one pot after long, slow cooking. Today's busy cooks know the reason they are so delicious—the flavours permeate the meat giving it special character of the herbs, wine and spices while it gently cooks. Best of all, all this can be happening while you put your feet up with a good book or whatever it is you want to do.

TODAY we enjoy a most diverse cooking culture, every community moving to a new country making its mark on what is eaten in their new home. Traditional to them, new and exotic to others. How does Tortoni with Olives strike you? Or Eight Treasure Soup? The Chinese consider eight a lucky number. Or exotic Laksa Lemak, or Tuna Carpaccio with Herbs?... and while thinking of carpaccio, there's Mango and Lime Carpaccio—delicious! When you fancy chicken, consider Couscous with Chicken Bedouin Style ... if it's roast lamb, try Moroccan Roast Lamb or M'Choui of Lamb. When there's a longing for a luscious dessert, Highland Mist with poached fruit evokes thoughts of Scotland, Chocolate Dacquoise takes us to Paris.

MANY traditional foods are given a new twist using today's top ingredients. Being a passionate cook, I like to choose the best-quality, freshest ingredients and produce wonderful dishes everyone will enjoy. I believe in the importance of variety, moderation and the use of premium and fresh foods in the diet. Nutritional research reinforces my belief that our future sense of well-being as individuals and as a family lies in our own hands. I want to encourage young people to cook and experienced cooks to enjoy cooking more. I want to encourage people to think of cooking as being a creative art, never a tiresome chore.

I WELCOME today's interest in good food, prepared in our own kitchens. The ultimate end to any day is sitting around your own table with your family and friends, enjoying time and food together—who could ask for anything more.

SHARE my passion for cooking; the rewards are manifold, not least its effect on those around us. A love of fine food turns children into little gourmets from their first solid bite. Discover the joy of new-found skills and new-found flavours. Like any other lively art or science or craft, cookery is continually evolving. It makes great sense to be part of it.

Margaret Fulton

MARGARET FULTON

LIGHT MEALS
AND STARTERS

THE sun is shining, the sky blue and cloudless, the water is sparkling. Will we have lunch in the cool of the house or will we take it to the garden and, in my case, enjoy the harbour with its myriad of sailing boats, ferry boats, tugs and canoes? When it is rainy, or a sou'wester is blowing, we light a fire and plan to sit around reading books and listening to music. I do believe we have tiny clocks in our bodies, clocks that ring little alarm bells with predictable regularity to say 'I feel peckish' or 'fiercely hungry' or even 'famished'. An enthusiastic cook immediately rises to the occasion.

YOU could start with a modest little soup using the stock an ardent cook always has on hand. It may be a soup rich and creamy, piping hot or chilled. A soup can be almost a meal in itself or the perfect starter. I can't think about soup without thinking what a good idea it is.

SALADS, too, give the passionate cook a chance to be creative. Although the most popular salad is tossed greens with a dressing of the best olive oil and a dash of vinegar, or a well-seasoned French dressing, we all make salads using cooked vegetables, cheese, meat or fish in different combinations.

VEGETABLES are very important; we enjoy making the most of them when they are in season. We look at the vast array of mushrooms—my local supplier keeps 14 different varieties and 18 varieties of potatoes. We get tropical, cold-weather and spring vegetables, roots and tubers. When artichokes, broad beans or exotic Asian vegetables appear, it is a challenge to buy them and create a great vegetable dish.

WHEN it is time for lunch, the passionate cook may plan on baking a fragrant warm bread or a crispy pizza. If friends are expected, it may inspire a layered lasagne made the modern way or a pasta salad. Why not try making lunch a time of enjoyment and relaxation? A time to indulge in your passion for cooking.

CHAPTER 1

SOUP'S ON!

Making soup is one of the most creative ways to cook. There are
vegetable soups, fragrant and full of flavour; fish soups, delicate and
creamy, or hot and spicy; meat and chicken soups; hot soups for a wintry
day and chilled soups for a hot summer's day. Soups can be hearty, a meal
in themselves, or a light beginning to a meal. Herbs, spices, brandy and
wine, along with the basic ingredients and a good bread,
all add flavour and excitement.

CHICKEN CORIANDER SOUP

*A beautiful spicy soup using fresh and dried spices, chicken breast and rice. You
may try using fresh (single, light) cream in place of coconut milk.*

INGREDIENTS

30 g (1 oz) butter

1 teaspoon ground coriander

1 teaspoon ground cumin

*1 chicken breast fillet (bone and
skin free), cut in cubes*

*2 tablespoons plain (all-purpose)
flour*

*5 cups (1.25 litres/2 imp. pints)
chicken stock (page 12), heated*

juice of ½ lemon

salt and freshly ground pepper

⅓ cup (90 mL/3 fl oz) coconut milk

¾ cup cooked rice

*½ cup fresh leafy coriander (Chinese
parsley) sprigs*

MELT the butter in a saucepan and stir in the ground coriander,
cumin and cubed chicken, cooking gently for 1 minute. Add the flour,
blend in and return to heat. Cook gently for another minute, then add
the stock. Stir until blended and cook a further 5–6 minutes. Add the
lemon juice, and salt and pepper to taste. Stir in the coconut milk and
the cooked rice. When the soup is heated through, add the coriander
sprigs and let it stand a minute or two before serving.

SERVES 6

COOKING RICE

*Bring 1 cup (250 mL/8 fl oz) water to the boil. Add a pinch of salt and
2 tablespoons rice, bring back to the boil. Reduce heat and cook until the
water evaporates, about 10–12 minutes. Turn off heat, cover and leave for
a further 5 minutes. Fluff up the rice before adding it to the soup.*

RIGHT: Chicken Coriander Soup calls for both fresh and ground coriander,
and a dash of lemon juice

STOCK, BROTH OR BOUILLON

Stock, broth or bouillon is the clear, flavourful liquid that you get after various meats and vegetables have been simmered in water and then strained. Stock made from beef is brown or light golden; poultry and veal make a white stock; fish a clear stock. Each one has its uses.

INGREDIENTS

1 kg (2 lb) beef bones (shank, marrow bone or rib bones)

500 g (1 lb) shin (fore shank) of beef, chopped

1 carrot, thickly sliced

1 onion, thickly sliced

2 teaspoons salt

1 teaspoon black peppercorns

bouquet garni

about 12 cups (3 litres/4¾ imp. pints) cold water (enough to cover the bones)

For making stock

Choose a saucepan with a flat base and a well-fitting lid. You don't want your precious liquid to evaporate too quickly and fill the kitchen with steam. In many recipes, a particular stock is called for—for example, chicken, meat or fish; where it is listed simply as 'stock' in the ingredients, use your own choice of chicken, beef or vegetable. Stock will keep for up to a week in the refrigerator, and it can also be frozen.

BEEF STOCK Put the bones into a large saucepan, then add the other ingredients and the bouquet garni. Cover with cold water. Bring slowly to the boil, skim the surface well, then simmer very gently, half-covered, for 3–4 hours. (Very slow simmering for a long time is the secret of well-flavoured stock.) Strain through a fine sieve, cool, then chill in the refrigerator. Remove the surface fat before using.

MAKES 12 CUPS

BROWN STOCK Make as above, but brown the bones in a baking dish in a preheated oven at 200°C (400°F) until bones and fatty bits are a deep brown. Proceed with recipe above.

VEAL STOCK Use veal shanks cut in pieces and make as for beef stock. This stock is used in brown sauces and soups; clarified, it is used in clear soups.

CHICKEN STOCK Make as for beef stock, using 1 kg (2 lb) raw fresh chicken bones (carcass, backs or wings)—your poultry supplier often has a bag of bone pieces at a very reasonable price.

VEGETABLE STOCK Make as for beef stock, omitting the beef bones and meat. Add 3 stalks diced celery, 1 chopped white turnip, 12 fresh parsley stems, 1 chopped small head of lettuce and a 2.5 cm (1 in.) piece of ginger.

THAI CHICKEN SOUP

This lovely, fragrant soup is called Tom Kha Gai.

INGREDIENTS

3 cups (750 mL/24 fl oz) chicken
stock

2 lemon grass stalks, tender parts
only, cut on bias

2 makrut or kaffir lime leaves

3 slices galangal, cut into julienne

6 mushrooms, sliced

½ teaspoon salt

3 tablespoons lime juice

2 tablespoons fish sauce (nam pla)

2 chicken breast fillets, cut into
strips

2 cups (500 mL/16 fl oz) coconut
milk

1–2 red chillies, split and seeded

PLACE the stock in a large saucepan. Add the lemon grass, lime leaves, galangal, mushrooms and salt, and bring slowly to the boil. Add the lime juice, fish sauce and chicken strips. Simmer, uncovered, for about 10 minutes, then add the coconut milk and chilli. Bring the soup slowly to the boil, stirring. Do not bring to the boil too quickly after adding the coconut milk, or the coconut milk will separate.

SERVES 6

KAFFIR LIME LEAVES

Makrut is the botanical name for kaffir lime in Thailand. Both fresh and dried kaffir lime leaves are available at many greengrocers and Asian stores, although it is preferable to use fresh. Lime leaves may be replaced with strips of lime rind.

HOT AND SOUR PRAWN SOUP

This hot, spicy soup with a sour tang is a favourite on Thai menus.

INGREDIENTS

12 large or 24 small prawns
(shrimp)

2 lemon grass stalks

4 makrut or kaffir lime leaves

4–5 mushrooms

2–3 tiny chillies, split and seeded

4 cups (1 litre/1¾ imp. pints)
chicken stock

4 tablespoons lime juice

2 tablespoons fish sauce (nam pla)

1 cup fresh coriander (Chinese
parsley) leaves

WASH the prawns, then peel them, but leave the tails on. Devein. Crush the tender white ends of the lemon grass, then slice the stalks finely, on the bias. Halve the lime leaves, then slice the mushrooms and chillies (use only 1 chilli if you don't like your dishes very hot).

HEAT the stock in a large saucepan. Add the lemon grass, lime leaves, mushrooms, chilli, lime juice and fish sauce. Bring the mixture to the boil, then reduce the heat and simmer for 2 minutes. Add the prawns and cook only until they turn pink, about 1 minute. Top with coriander leaves.

SERVES 4–6

NOTE If kaffir lime leaves are unavailable or hard to find, use a strip of lime rind instead.

SPINACH AND CHICKEN SOUP

A light, oriental-style soup like this is the perfect start to a meal.
The aromatic and pungent flavours of garlic, ginger, chilli and sesame are
just enough to sharpen your appetite, yet the soup is very light.
The tender spinach hardly needs cooking, the leaves just
soften in the simmering stock. Remove chilli before eating if preferred.
If you don't have time to make the chicken dumplings, finely cut up
2 chicken breasts instead.

CHICKEN DUMPLINGS

1 medium-size chicken breast fillet

salt and freshly ground black pepper

1 egg white

2 teaspoons cornflour (cornstarch)

½ teaspoon chopped fresh ginger

¼ fresh red chilli, chopped

1 teaspoon sesame oil

SOUP

2 leeks

1 bunch spinach

1 tablespoon olive oil

1 clove garlic, peeled and chopped

2 small chillies, sliced in two
* lengthwise and seeded*

2.5 cm (1 in.) piece of fresh ginger,
* peeled and finely chopped*

5 cups (1.25 litres/2 imp. pints)
* chicken stock*

salt and freshly ground black pepper

sesame oil

TO MAKE the chicken dumplings, finely chop the chicken fillet or process it in a food processor until finely chopped. Season with salt and pepper, add the egg white and beat well, then add the cornflour, ginger, chilli and sesame oil, and beat to a paste. Using two teaspoons, shape the mixture into 12 small, olive shapes. To do this, scoop up a rounded spoonful of mixture and, with the other teaspoon, scoop the mixture out. Place on baking parchment or a plate and chill until required.

TO MAKE the soup, wash the leeks thoroughly of any sand and grit, and cut the white part and some of the green into fine rings. Wash the spinach well and remove the stems. Shake the leaves, stack them and cut into shreds. Set aside.

HEAT the oil in a large saucepan over a low heat and add the garlic, chilli, ginger and leeks, and cook gently for about 5 minutes. Add the chicken stock and simmer for 5 minutes. Drop the chicken dumpling balls into the soup and simmer for 2 minutes. Add the spinach and bring back to the boil. Season to taste with salt and pepper. To serve, pour immediately into deep Chinese-type soup bowls. Top each serving with a splash of sesame oil.

SERVES 6

RIGHT: Spinach and Chicken Soup
with fresh ginger and sesame oil for
oriental flavour

ORIENTAL SALMON SOUP

This is an East meets West dish, using beautiful Atlantic salmon and cooking it in a Western way, but with Asian coconut and ginger. Thai green curry paste may be added for a spicy finish; this is available in jars and cans from most delicatessens.

INGREDIENTS

1 piece Atlantic salmon, about
  1.25 kg (2½ lb)

3 tablespoons butter

1 leek, washed and finely sliced

1 clove garlic, chopped

2.5 cm (1 in.) piece of green ginger,
  peeled and cut julienne

6 cups (1.5 litres/2½ imp. pints) fish
  stock (page 130)

1 teaspoon salt

freshly ground black pepper

12 tender spinach leaves, washed
  and trimmed

1 tablespoon plain (all-purpose)
  flour

½ cup (125 mL/4 fl oz) coconut milk

1 teaspoon Thai green curry paste
  (optional)

3 tablespoons torn fresh chervil or
  coriander (Chinese parsley) sprigs

REMOVE the skin from the salmon and cut into 4 fillets. Set the fillets aside. In a saucepan, heat 2 tablespoons of the butter and sweat the leeks with the garlic and ginger over a gentle heat, shaking the pan occasionally. When the leeks are soft, add the fish stock, salt and pepper to taste. Bring to the boil, reduce heat and simmer, covered, for about 10 minutes. Add the spinach and cook for 1–2 minutes. Meanwhile, knead together the remaining 1 tablespoon butter and the flour; lightly whisk bits of this into the liquid over a gentle heat to thicken the soup slightly.

PLACE the salmon fillets in the pan and spoon soup over them. Bring to the simmer and poach the fish about 4 minutes, or until opaque and firm.

USING a slotted spoon, lift the spinach and the salmon onto 4 heated, flattish soup bowls. Bring the soup just back to the boil. Lightly stir in the coconut milk and Thai green curry paste (if using), and ladle the soup over the salmon in bowls. Scatter with the chervil or coriander, and serve.

SERVES 4

ATLANTIC SALMON

To remove the skin from the fillets, lay skin side down on a board and, with a sharp knife, separate skin from flesh, pulling the skin gently and easing the flesh with the knife.

This lovely soup is great for family meals or entertaining, the soup base being at the ready for the final cooking of the spinach and the poaching of the fish. When large salmon trout (rainbow trout raised in sea farms) are available, you can use them as they are very close to Atlantic salmon.

TARRAGON SOUP

This soup gained the name Mary Queen of Scots soup after Mary, returning from France in 1561 to rule Scotland, introduced 'estragon' to her country men. The infusion of fresh and dried tarragon gives sophistication to chicken soup.

INGREDIENTS

4 cups (1 litre/1¾ imp. pints) strong chicken stock (page 12)

6 sprigs tarragon, leaves removed and stalks set aside

1 teaspoon dried tarragon

2 tablespoons butter

1 tablespoon plain (all-purpose) flour

¼ cup (60 mL/2 fl oz) fresh (single, light) cream

1 tablespoon lemon juice

salt and freshly ground black pepper

HEAT the stock and add the dried tarragon and stalks with half the tarragon leaves. Bring to the boil, then cover the saucepan and simmer for 5 minutes. Remove from the heat for 20 minutes.

MELT the butter in a saucepan, add the flour and stir until blended to a smooth paste. Pour on the strained stock through a sieve and simmer for 3–4 minutes, stirring all the time. When smooth and blended, add the cream, stirring gently. Add the lemon juice and salt and pepper to taste. Chop the remaining tarragon leaves and scatter over the top. Let stand for a few minutes before serving.

SERVES 4–6

SWEET POTATO SOUP

Two varieties of vegetable—root and tuber—are used in this intriguing soup. For an earthy, rustic flavour, choose old potatoes or one of the yellow-fleshed varieties such as desirée and red-skinned sweet potato or golden kumera.

INGREDIENTS

45 g (1½ oz) butter

2 potatoes, peeled and diced

1 yellow sweet potato, peeled and diced

salt and ground nutmeg, to taste

4 cups (1 litre/1¾ imp. pints) water or chicken stock (page 12)

¾ cup (185 mL/6 fl oz) milk

3 tablespoons fresh chervil sprigs or coriander (Chinese parsley)

2 tablespoons (single, light) cream

MELT the butter in a heavy saucepan. Put in the potatoes and cook very gently in the butter for 10 minutes until they begin to soften— they must not brown. Sprinkle with a little salt and a grating or pinch of nutmeg. Pour in the water or chicken stock, cover the pan and let the potatoes simmer for 20–25 minutes.

SIEVE or purée the potato mixture in a blender or food processor. Return to the rinsed pan. Add the milk, which has been brought to the boil in another pan—this is important for a light finish. Before serving, stir in the chervil or coriander, and the cream.

SERVES 4–6

WINTER SOUP

Almost everybody has a winter craving for a hearty, wholesome soup.

INGREDIENTS

¼ cup (60 mL/2 fl oz) olive oil

2 carrots, diced

2 medium potatoes, peeled and
　　diced

1 leek (white parts and a little
　　green), well washed and sliced

2 small stalks celery, diced

1 small onion, chopped

1 cup (185 g/6 oz) shelled green
　　peas, fresh or frozen

8 cups (2 litres/3¼ imp. pints) hot
　　vegetable stock or water

1 × 500 g (1 lb) can cannellini
　　beans, drained

8 spinach leaves, shredded

salt and freshly ground pepper

toasted bread slices, grated
　　Parmesan cheese and extra virgin
　　olive oil, to serve

HEAT the olive oil in a large saucepan and gently sauté the vegetables, except the spinach, for about 15 minutes. Add the hot stock or water, bring slowly to the boil and simmer very gently for about 20 minutes. (Cook the vegetables longer if you prefer them not so firm.) Add the drained beans and spinach, and simmer for a further 5 minutes. Season to taste.

SERVE very hot, ladled over the toasted bread slices or serve bread separately. Sprinkle each bowl with plenty of grated Parmesan. Finish off with a trickle of olive oil; it adds flavour and softens the finish.

SERVES 6

NOTE The vegetables may be varied and you can use red kidney beans, borlotti beans or haricot beans. The olive oil is passed with the soup—each diner adds as much as they want. Use the best extra virgin olive oil you can buy.

PISTOU

Prepare winter soup as above without the Parmesan. Finish with the toasted bread on the side, and serve the soup with a swirl of pistou.

PISTOU

1 cup fresh basil leaves

4 cloves garlic, peeled

1 large tomato, peeled, halved and
　　seeded

1 tablespoon tomato paste

½ cup (60 g/2 oz) grated Parmesan
　　cheese

3 tablespoons olive oil

MAKE the pistou by blending the basil with the garlic in a food processor or blender. Add the tomato, tomato paste and Parmesan cheese. Purée to a paste, adding the oil gradually. Stir the pistou into the soup just before serving or allow guests to serve themselves. Serve piping hot with toasted bread slices.

LEFT: Winter Soup is finished with a good olive oil and Parmesan cheese, or perhaps Pistou

TOMATO SAFFRON SOUP

Vermouth, with its infusion of aged wine and herbs add subtlety to this soup

INGREDIENTS

6 red vine-ripened tomatoes, peeled
and seeded
½ cup (125 mL/4 fl oz) dry
vermouth
⅛ teaspoon saffron threads
30 g (1 oz) butter
1 medium onion, sliced
5 cups (1.25 litres/2 imp. pints)
vegetable stock or water
1 bay leaf
1 teaspoon granulated sugar
pinch of ground nutmeg
salt and freshly ground pepper
1 teaspoon cornflour (cornstarch)
1 tablespoon water
2 tablespoons chopped parsley

CHOP all the tomatoes but the last one; dice this and set aside. Combine the vermouth and saffron, and set aside. Melt the butter in a saucepan, add the onion, cover and soften for 5–6 minutes. Remove from the heat, add the chopped tomatoes, stock, bay leaf, sugar, nutmeg and salt and pepper to taste. Stir until boiling, then simmer for 10–15 minutes.

RUB through a sieve, pour back into rinsed pan, and reheat. Adjust seasoning and thicken slightly with a teaspoonful or more of cornflour blended with the water. Add the vermouth and saffron, and the reserved diced tomato. Heat gently. Serve ladled into heated bowls with the diced tomato and parsley.

SERVES 6

SAFFRON
Saffron is a rare spice, expensive but worth it. The dried stigmas of the Crocus sativus *give it an exotic flavour that is very agreeable.*

SORREL SOUP

Try if possible to use sorrel with its fresh lemony tang, but if
unavailable make it with tender young spinach.

INGREDIENTS

60 g (2 oz) butter
20 sorrel leaves, washed and
trimmed, plus 6–8 extra, shredded
1 leek, washed and finely sliced
salt and freshly ground pepper
3 potatoes, peeled and diced
5 cups (1.25 litres/2 imp. pints)
chicken stock
1 cup (250 mL/8 fl oz) milk or fresh
(single, light) cream, hot
a sprinkling of chopped parsley

MELT half the butter in a large saucepan. Add the 20 sorrel leaves and the leek. Cook over a low heat until soft, without colouring. Season with salt and pepper, and add the potato. Stir in the chicken stock, cover and simmer gently for about 20 minutes.

SIEVE or purée the potato mixture in a blender or food processor. Reheat in a clean pan. Melt the remaining butter in a small saucepan, add the extra sorrel and cook slowly until most of the moisture has evaporated, about 5 minutes. Add to the soup, then blend in the hot milk or cream, and adjust seasoning. Reheat, but do not boil. Serve immediately, sprinkled with the parsley.

SERVES 6

ALMOND SOUP

A Spanish soup enjoyed chilled in the summer time, hot in the winter. You can use store-bought ground almonds, but they tend to give a grainy finish so that the soup needs to be put through a fine sieve.

INGREDIENTS

¾ cup (125g/4 oz) almonds, blanched and skinned

1 clove garlic, peeled

3 cups (750 mL/24 fl oz) chicken stock

1 small onion, stuck with 2 cloves

1 bay leaf

pinch of ground nutmeg

salt and freshly ground black pepper

30 g (1 oz) butter

2 tablespoons plain (all-purpose) flour

1 cup (250 mL/8 fl oz) fresh (single, light) cream

USING a mortar and pestle, pound the almonds and garlic to a smooth paste, or purée in an electric blender. Combine the ground almonds, stock, onion and bay leaf in a saucepan. Simmer, covered, for 20 minutes. Remove the onion and bay leaf, pour mixture into a jug and add nutmeg and salt and pepper to taste. Melt the butter in a saucepan, add the flour and stir over a low heat; blend in the stock mixture. Stir over the heat until boiling. Simmer for 5 minutes. Add the cream and reheat, but do not boil. Serve cold or hot, with a sprinkle of slivered almonds and some fresh grapes in season.

SERVES 4

NOTE Toasted slivered almonds and a few grapes make a delightful garnish for this soup. Chill grapes for cold soup.

CHILLED BORSCH

A clear, chilled borsch, when made with excellent stock, will jell slightly. The egg whites assure you of a ruby clear soup.

INGREDIENTS

4 cups (1 litre/1¾ imp. pints) strong beef stock

4 raw beetroot (red beets), peeled and grated

½ cup (125 mL/4 fl oz) red wine

2 tablespoons tomato paste

2 bay leaves

2 egg whites, stiffly beaten

grated rind of 1 lemon

salt

pinch of cayenne pepper

5 tablespoons sour cream

PUT the stock in a large saucepan. Add the beetroot, wine, tomato paste, bay leaves and egg whites. Beat over a moderate heat until borsch comes to the boil, then draw off heat and leave for 10 minutes. Pour through a colander lined with a fine damp cloth and place in the refrigerator until cold. Add the lemon rind, salt and cayenne pepper to the sour cream and serve separately, with guests spooning some into their own bowls.

SERVES 4–6

EIGHT TREASURE SOUP

Numbers have always been significant to the Chinese. I loved the name and make this delicious soup after a visit to Chinatown when I pick up Chinese delicacies. I try to put eight treasures into the soup as eight is considered lucky, making the soup precious.

INGREDIENTS

250 g (8 oz) Chinese barbecue pork, sliced

250 g (8 oz) Chinese roast duck, sliced

6 cups (1.5 litres/2½ imp. pints) chicken stock

8 Chinese won ton (dumplings) or bean curd, cubed

60 g (2 oz) thin rice noodles

4–6 Chinese chard (bok choy) or Chinese broccoli (gai larn), quartered

8–10 green prawns (shrimp), peeled, deveined and tails intact

2.5 cm (1 in.) piece of fresh ginger, cut into julienne

3–4 spring onions (scallions), sliced on the diagonal

SEASONINGS

1 teaspoon granulated sugar
salt and freshly ground black pepper
1 teaspoon sesame oil
side dishes of soy sauce, sesame oil and hot chilli sauce

PUT the barbecue pork and roast duck in a heavy pan over a gentle heat to heat through. In a separate saucepan, bring the chicken stock to a boil. Add the won ton dumplings or bean curd, bring stock back to the boil, then add the noodles and bring to the boil once more, before adding the chard. Bring back to the boil and then add the prawns and ginger. Season the soup with the seasonings.

LADLE the soup into 4 shallow soup bowls, carefully arranging the ingredients to distribute them evenly. Place portions of barbecued pork and duck in plates and top with a sprinkling of sliced green shallot. Serve tiny bowls of soy sauce, sesame oil and hot chilli sauce alongside the soup; guests can dip pieces of food to individual taste.

SERVES 4

KNOW YOUR NOODLES

Thick Rice Sticks: *made from rice flour and water. To cook, cover rice sticks with boiling water, soak until softened, about 20 minutes, then drain.*

Thin Rice Sticks (Rice Vermicelli): *made from rice flour and water. To cook, cover with boiling water for 3–5 minutes, then drain. Add to soup and continue to boil for a further 3 minutes.*

Egg Noodles: *round, yellow noodles. To cook, pour enough boiling water over noodles to cover. Leave to stand for a few minutes, then drain.*

Cellophane Noodles (Bean Thread): *made from green mung bean. These are already cooked, so soak the noodles in hot water for 10 minutes, drain and rinse.*

RIGHT: Eight Treasure Soup—add your own choice of noodles and treasures

CHAPTER 2

SUMMER AND WINTER SALADS

'A day without greens is a day without sunshine' and that's how I feel about fresh salads. In a country where wonderfully inexpensive vegetables and fruits, fresh herbs, fish, seafood, poultry and nuts are grown in abundance, and superb cheeses, oils and olives are readily available, we can with imagination create salads that will provide that glorious feeling of sunshine.

CLASSIC VINAIGRETTE

The classic vinaigrette or French dressing is a subtle mixture of good-quality olive oil, wine vinegar, salt and pepper. To this mixture, Dijon mustard, garlic and fresh herbs may be added. Vinaigrette can be used as a dressing for salads, cooked vegetables, pasta and rice salads.

INGREDIENTS

1 tablespoon good vinegar

¼ teaspoon salt

freshly ground black pepper

1 teaspoon Dijon mustard

4 tablespoons olive oil

VINAIGRETTE VARIES WITH ITS USE
For a light, delicate salad, mix the dressing just enough to create a liaison; for a more robust dressing, add the oil drop by drop and the mixture will thicken. A tiny dab of harissa, Tabasco sauce or chilli gives a zippy hot dressing. A teaspoon of balsamic vinegar gives an intriguing sharp taste.

PUT the vinegar into a small bowl with the salt, pepper and mustard. Mix well with a fork or whisk, and slowly add the oil, beating until the mixture thickens slightly. If the dressing tastes sharp, add more oil or a pinch of caster (superfine) sugar. If the dressing is too oily for your taste, add more salt. An alternative method is to combine all the ingredients in a glass jar, cover and shake well until the mixture thickens.

MAKES ABOUT ½ CUP

HOT VINAIGRETTE I like to add a hot vinaigrette to steamed potatoes or warm poached fish, meat or poultry served with crisp salad greens. Make as for Classic Vinaigrette, but heat the oil, vinegar, some chopped golden shallot and pepper, and whisk in the mustard. Spoon over warm salad and toss lightly.

MAYONNAISE

Homemade mayonnaise, with its sumptuous texture and fresh, subtle flavour, is one of the great sauces. It takes only about 10 minutes to make by hand once you have mastered the technique and is faster still with a food processor.

INGREDIENTS

2 egg yolks

½ teaspoon salt

pinch of white pepper

½ teaspoon dry mustard or

1 teaspoon Dijon mustard

2 teaspoons vinegar or lemon juice

1 cup (250 mL/8 fl oz) olive oil or salad oil or a mixture of both

---

MAYONNAISE

Mayonnaise, so the story goes, was created by Cardinal Richelieu in the 17th century. It is interesting that it is still made the same way today, except that one may, using great care, combine the emulsion with an electric beater or food processor instead of a wire whisk. Master the skill of making this sauce in the old way (with a wire whisk) before making it with electric beaters.

CURDLED MAYONNAISE

If either handmade or machine-made mayonnaise refuses to thicken, or if it curdles, take a clean, warmed bowl and beat an egg yolk with ½ teaspoon each of salt and vinegar. Gradually beat in the curdled mayonnaise—very slowly at first and then more quickly.

HAVE the ingredients at room temperature. Warm the eggs and oil in hot water if they are cold. Rinse out a mixing bowl with hot water and wrap a damp cloth around the base to keep it steady.

PLACE the egg yolks, salt, pepper, mustard and 1 teaspoon vinegar or lemon juice in the bowl and beat with a wire whisk to combine. When thick, begin to add the oil, drop by drop, whisking constantly and incorporating each addition thoroughly before adding the next. As the mixture thickens, the oil flow can be increased to a steady, thin stream, but you must keep beating constantly. When all the oil is incorporated, beat in the remaining vinegar or lemon juice. Store in a cool place, covered.

MAKES ABOUT 1 CUP

FOOD PROCESSOR OR BLENDER MAYONNAISE
Place 1 egg yolk and 1 whole egg, salt, pepper, mustard and 1 teaspoon vinegar or lemon juice in the bowl and blend for a few seconds. With the motor running, add the oil gradually, ensuring that each addition has been absorbed before adding more. When all the oil has been incorporated, blend in the remaining vinegar or lemon juice.

GARLIC MAYONNAISE OR AIOLI Crush 2 or 3 cloves garlic to a paste with the salt in a bowl. Add the egg yolks and pepper, mustard and vinegar or lemon juice, and mix until thick, then add the oil as for the basic recipe. Do not add too much lemon or vinegar. Serve with boiled meats, fish and cold cooked or raw vegetables.

REMOULADE SAUCE To ½ cup (4½ fl oz) of mayonnaise add 1 good teaspoon French or Dijon mustard and 1 tablespoon each of chopped gherkins, capers and parsley, and a teaspoon of tarragon all mixed together. When thoroughly combined, stir in a few drops of anchovy essence (extract). Serve with egg salads, fish, prawns (shrimp) and pigs' trotters.

BASIL MAYONNAISE Shred 8–10 fresh basil leaves and fold into ½ cup mayonnaise.

MOROCCAN SALAD

Fresh salads precede most meals in Morocco and are more like Italian antipasti, designed to inspire the appetite and refresh the palate. They are beautifully seasoned with unexpected flavours and contrasts. Such things as carrots, beetroots, radish with lemon juice and sometimes orange juice are finished off with a sprinkling of cumin. Of course, good olives and olive oil are always in evidence. Here are two salads that make an inviting platter, although a small salad of either may be your choice.

INGREDIENTS

2 red radishes, sliced or diced

1 continental cucumber, peeled, seeded and diced

1 small red salad onion, thinly sliced or diced

salt

1 clove garlic, peeled

2 tablespoons fresh lemon juice

3 tablespoons extra virgin olive oil

freshly ground black pepper, to taste

½ cup fresh mint leaves, torn

1 cup rocket (arugula) leaves, cut in two if large

2 red vine-ripened tomatoes, peeled, seeded and diced

12 small black olives, pitted

1 lemon, quartered

a few mint sprigs

SPRINKLE the radishes, cucumber and onion with salt and allow to stand for 5 minutes in a salad bowl.

CHOP the garlic with ¼ teaspoon salt. Stir in the lemon juice, olive oil and pepper. Add the mint and rocket to the radishes, cucumber and onion. Pour the lemon juice mixture over the top. Toss the ingredients in the bowl, cover with plastic wrap and refrigerate for up to 2 hours. Just before serving, stir in the chopped tomatoes. Garnish with the olives and lemon, and a few mint sprigs.

SERVES 4–6

SHREDDED MOROCCAN SALAD Using one of the finest shredding blades of a plastic or wooden mandolin, shred 1 carrot, 1 beetroot (red beet) and ½ large white radish, keeping them in separate piles. Make small mounds of each vegetable on a platter, squeeze generously with a dressing of lemon juice and olive oil, and sprinkle lightly with ground cumin. Lemon or orange wedges can be used to garnish the salads; some people like to squeeze the juice over the salad.

NOTE I use a fine julienne shredder and find it very useful for garnishes and salad making.

RIGHT: Moroccan Salad, composed of colourful Mediterrean vegetables, is surrounded by the Shredded Moroccan Salad with a fresh, spiced dressing

WARM CHICKEN WALNUT SALAD

A kind of East meets West salad finished with a warm dressing.

INGREDIENTS

2 tablespoons light soy sauce

3 tablespoons dry white wine

1 teaspoon dried tarragon

1 teaspoon dry mustard

3 boneless chicken fillets

mixed salad greens

2 tablespoons toasted walnuts

WALNUT DRESSING

1 tablespoon walnut oil

4–5 drops sesame oil

2 tablespoons olive oil

1 tablespoon orange juice

1 teaspoon chopped fresh tarragon

salt and freshly ground pepper

COMBINE the soy sauce, wine, tarragon and mustard. Marinate the chicken in this mixture for 1–2 hours. Grill the chicken breasts gently under a preheated grill (broiler) for 5 minutes each side, basting with a little marinade from time to time, or cook on a heated ribbed grill. Remove from the heat and brush all over with marinade. Allow to cool a little. Cut each chicken fillet into long thin slices. Arrange a little pile of salad greens on 4 plates. Place the warm chicken in a fan shape on top and strew with walnuts, which may be broken into pieces.

TO MAKE the dressing, combine the ingredients in a bowl and beat lightly to combine. Heat gently and spoon the dressing over each serving of salad.

SERVES 4

MINTED PRAWN SALAD

The complex seasonings of Thai cooking intrigue almost everyone who has sampled it.

INGREDIENTS

750 g (1½ lb) green prawns (shrimp)

1 teaspoon fish sauce (nam pla)

juice of 1 lime

4 tablespoons coconut milk

2 teaspoons sugar

½ teaspoon Thai green curry paste

2 cloves garlic, peeled and crushed

6 slices fresh ginger, cut julienne

½–1 fresh red chilli, sliced

freshly ground black pepper

8–10 fresh mint leaves

1 punnet green pea shoots

PEEL the prawns, leaving tails intact, devein and wash thoroughly. Mix the fish sauce, lime juice, coconut milk, sugar, green curry paste, garlic, ginger, chilli and pepper in a bowl. Drop the prawns into a pan of simmering, salted water for 1 minute or until they turn pink. Lift out and toss in the dressing; add the mint leaves and toss. If serving as a salad, make a mound of pea shoots or greens on 6 serving plates and top with prawns. To serve as a main course, serve with steamed jasmine rice (page 10).

SERVES 6

NOTE The prawns may vary in size; use what seem best at the market place. If prawns or shrimp are tiny, remove heads and tails, peel, devein and wash thoroughly.

SEAFOOD AND MESCLUN SALAD WITH ARTICHOKE DRESSING

The first time I was served this salad, I thought how fresh and light looking it was. As I started to enjoy the greens, I came across a still warm, delicate scallop, then I became aware of a delicious dressing—artichokes, I detected. I've been making it at home ever since and it's always a delight. Serve as a light first course; vary with pretty pink prawns (shrimp).

INGREDIENTS

1 teaspoon balsamic vinegar

salt and freshly ground pepper

1 tablespoon extra virgin olive oil

8 radicchio leaves, rinsed and dried, torn into 2 or 3 pieces

250 g (8 oz) mesclun or mixed salad greens

18 scallops or raw king prawns (shrimp)

2 teaspoons olive oil

DRESSING

3–4 drained marinated artichoke hearts in olive oil

1 tablespoon sherry vinegar or red wine vinegar

1 tablespoon fresh lemon juice

salt and freshly ground black pepper

4 tablespoons olive oil, preferably virgin

2 tablespoons warm water

IN A large bowl, whisk together the vinegar and salt and pepper to taste. Add the oil in a stream, whisking until the dressing is lightly emulsified. Toss the radicchio and mesclun with this dressing.

REMOVE any brown from the scallops; if using prawns, peel and devein. Heat the oil in a frying pan and add the scallops or prawns, toss lightly just until they change colour—the scallops creamy white, the prawns a pretty pink. Set aside while making the dressing.

TO MAKE the dressing, purée the artichoke hearts with the vinegar, lemon juice and salt and pepper to taste in an electric blender or food processor. With the motor running, add the oil in a stream and then the warm water, blending the mixture well.

DIVIDE the greens among 4 or 6 plates; divide the seafood among the salad, scattering it neatly on the bed of greens. Drizzle the salad with the artichoke dressing. Serve with crusty bread if liked.

SERVES 4–6

DEVEINING PRAWNS

Make a slit down the back of each and remove the back intestinal tract with a toothpick or point of a paring knife, or insert a metal skewer under the back vein and gently remove. Rinse and pat dry.

GRILLED RED CAPSICUMS

This is a Spanish version of capsicum (sweet pepper) salad found throughout the Mediterranean. Lovely with chunks of crusty farmhouse bread.

INGREDIENTS

2 red and 2 yellow capsicums (sweet
   peppers), quartered, seeds and ribs
   removed
2 tablespoons olive oil
½ cup (75 g/2½ oz) black olives
   (kalamata or small niçoise olives)
1 clove garlic, chopped
1 tablespoon small capers, drained
fresh herbs such as parsley, oregano,
   chives and basil, torn
salt and freshly ground black pepper
balsamic vinegar, to taste

LAY the capsicum quarters out, skin side up on a grilling tray and roast under a red-hot grill (broiler) until the skin is blistered. Remove the skins, then rinse flesh under a cold tap. Cut each quarter into two or three strips and place them in a shallow serving dish. Heat the olive oil, olives, garlic, capers and herbs in a pan, tossing lightly for only an instant. Add the salt and pepper to taste and a dash of balsamic vinegar, and spoon over the capsicums. Cover and let stand for 5 minutes before serving.

SERVES 4–6

PANZANELLA

This Tuscan bread salad, of which there are many versions, is at its best when made with sun-ripened bright tomatoes; a can of the best tuna fish, packed in oil; extra virgin olive oil from Tuscany and some brine-cured green or black olives. Use Italian crusty bread or a good French levain, *a type of sourdough bread.*

INGREDIENTS

4 thick slices crusty bread
3 red tomatoes, cored and diced
1 red salad onion, finely sliced
1 × 185 g (6 oz) can tuna
⅓ cup (60 g/2 oz) black olives
1 cup fresh basil leaves
⅓ cup (90 mL/3 fl oz) extra virgin
   olive oil
1–2 tablespoons wine vinegar
4 cloves garlic, finely chopped
salt and freshly ground pepper

CUT or break the bread slices in two or in chunky pieces. Place in a large bowl with the tomatoes and onion rings, then the tuna—the tuna can be broken into chunks. Toss lightly then add olives, basil and garlic. Season to taste then sprinkle with olive oil and vinegar, toss lightly then allow to stand for 15 minutes for flavours to blend. Transfer to large plates.

SERVES 4–6

STORING TOMATOES If possible, buy firm vine-ripened tomatoes. Store at room temperature for the best flavour.

LEFT: Grilled Red Capsicums are dressed with good olive oil, olives, capers and fresh herbs—a superb first course

POTATO SALAD

I learned to make a good potato salad from a master French chef. It changed my mind about potato salads, which had been rather stodgy and often clammy and cold. The first thing is the choice of potato. Today there are many remarkably good ones available—pink fir apple potatoes, pink-eyes with yellow flesh, baby new potatoes and kipflers. Mayonnaise may be spooned over the top. Importantly, it is served at room temperature.

INGREDIENTS

750 g (1½ lb) potatoes such as
   kipfler, pink-eye or pink fir apple
salted water
1 teaspoon salt
freshly ground black pepper
2–3 tablespoons good wine vinegar
6–7 tablespoons extra virgin
   olive oil
4 tablespoons stock or hot water
fresh parsley, chives, chervil and
   tarragon, chopped
3–4 spring onions (scallions),
   chopped (optional, for a more
   pungent salad)
½–¾ cup (125–185 mL/4–6 fl oz)
   mayonnaise (optional) (page 25)
extra chopped fresh parsley, to
   garnish

BOIL the potatoes, unpeeled, in salted water to cover until they are tender. Drain, peel and cut into thick slices. Spread over a shallow dish. While the potatoes are still hot, season with the salt and a little pepper. Beat the vinegar and oil together well with a fork. Sprinkle over the potatoes. Add the chopped herbs to taste and spring onions (if using). Let the salad stand at room temperature until most of the liquid is absorbed. Turn the potato slices carefully to ensure even seasoning. Serve the salad without chilling. For a creamy salad, spoon the mayonnaise over the potatoes. Top with the extra chopped parsley.

SERVES 4–6

POTATO AND EGG MAYONNAISE Make potato salad as above. Before adding the mayonnaise, top with 4 hard-boiled eggs (page 36), halved. Spoon mayonnaise over. For a festive finish, soak 8 anchovy fillets in milk for 20 minutes, then drain. Slit in two lengthwise and arrange on top in lattice fashion; set a black olive in each diamond of anchovy. Sprinkle with chopped parsley.

FOR A LIGHTER TOPPING, combine ¾ cup (185 mL/6 fl oz) mayonnaise with ¼ cup (60 mL/2 fl oz) fresh (single, light) cream and 1 teaspoon Worcestershire sauce. Spoon the mayonnaise over the egg and sprinkle with paprika.

POTATOES WITH RED CAPSICUMS Make potato salad as above, mask with mayonnaise. Take 2 whole red capsicums (sweet peppers) and grill (broil) until the skins turn black and will flake off. This takes about 15 minutes; they should be turned as soon as one side is done. When cool, peel off the skin, take out the seeds and wash the flesh under a cold tap. Cut into strips and arrange the strips around or in a lattice fashion on top of the potatoes. Sprinkle generously with chopped parsley.

RHINELAND HERRING AND POTATO SALAD Make a
potato salad as on page 32. Add 1 cup diced, cooked beetroot, 1 large
apple, cored and diced, and 3–4 diced, pickled herrings (these can be
bought in jars or canned). Combine and finish off with a topping of
chopped parsley or dill just before serving. Half a cup (125 mL/4 fl oz)
of sour cream is sometimes folded in.

ROCKET AND POTATO SALAD

*If you have taken to the nippy taste of fresh rocket (arugula), there is no
simpler or better way of enjoying it than with a warm potato salad
with a creamy mustard dressing.*

INGREDIENTS

*375 g (¾ lb) small new potatoes,
 washed*

1 large egg yolk

1 tablespoon coarse-grain mustard

1 tablespoon white wine vinegar

sea salt

5 tablespoons olive oil

2 golden shallots, sliced

1–2 bunches of rocket (arugula)

2 tablespoons chopped parsley

GARNISHES

*This salad may be garnished with
a twist of grilled capsicum (sweet
pepper), a curl of anchovy, a few
black olives, a few bright cherry
tomatoes or yellow teardrop
(pear) tomatoes.*

IN A steamer set over boiling water, steam the new potatoes, covered,
for 18–20 minutes. Lift out to cool just enough to handle. Meanwhile,
in a small bowl, whisk the egg yolk with the mustard until it thickens.
Add the vinegar and salt, and then the oil, dropping it in a slow
stream, whisking until the mixture forms a thickish emulsion. Add the
golden shallots.

PEEL the potatoes, although this is not necessary, and cut each in
three or four slices. Put in a bowl while still warm with the dressing.
Let stand for 10 minutes.

WASH the rocket, swooshing the leaves around in water. Shake well,
cut off tough stems and pat dry in absorbent paper towels. Arrange
rocket on 4 plates, top with potato salad and garnish with parsley.

SERVES 4

BLACK AND WHITE WINTER SALAD

One of the joys of winter is the appearance of the lovely Florence fennel (finocchio) with its exotic anise flavour, and the bittersweet witlof (Belgian endive). Witlof's pearly-pale spear-shaped leaves may be cut into julienne, sliced across forming crescents or left whole.

INGREDIENTS

1 medium Florence fennel (finocchio) bulb

3 witlofs (Belgian endives)

½ red salad onion, sliced very thinly (optional)

2 tablespoons black olives, washed

1 piece Parmigiano-Reggiano cheese, about 185 g (6 oz)

GREEN PEPPERCORN DRESSING

3 tablespoons extra virgin olive oil

1 tablespoon fresh lemon juice

1 clove garlic, finely chopped

½ teaspoon green peppercorns

½ teaspoon sea salt

TRIM the fennel, discarding stalks and root base, halve and cut into thin slices lengthwise. Cut the witlof into long, thin matchsticks. Lightly pile the fennel and witlof on a platter, or on 6 dinner plates. Scatter with the onion rings (if using) and black olives. Using a cheese plane or vegetable peeler, shave off thin slices of cheese, using only half the cheese (keep remaining cheese for other uses). Scatter over the salad.

IN A small bowl, whisk together the dressing ingredients. Drizzle the salad with the dressing.

SERVES 6

SLICING FENNEL

To get fine, matchstick slices of fennel, which make the salad light and tender, halve the bulb. Using a mandolin fitted with a julienne blade, cut the fennel in thin strips. Alternatively, use a very sharp knife.

WITLOF

Select the pearly witlof for this salad. It is also available with rosy pink tips, which are delicious in salads, but would change the look of this salad.

RIGHT: Black and White Winter Salad combines Florence fennel with its sweet aniseed flavours and the delicately bitter flavour of witlof. A lovely combination—black olives add drama

SALADE MAISON

A salad like this makes a fabulous meal on its own, either for an evening meal or a weekend luncheon. It is a regular in my house. Like many good salads, it is made with ingredients on hand and in season. Raw vegetables, garlic, boiled new potatoes or cooked white beans, cooked green beans, hard-boiled eggs and olives are used.

INGREDIENTS

500 g (1 lb) tuna cooked in oil or
  2 × 210 g (7 oz) cans

light olive oil, to cover

a few lemony herbs, such as lemon thyme, lemon balm or citrus leaves

500 g (1 lb) new potatoes, scrubbed, but unpeeled

4 large eggs, at room temperature

500 g (1 lb) green beans, ends trimmed

1 Cos (romaine) lettuce or *bunch of spinach, washed and dried*

3 tomatoes, each cut into eights

¾ cup (125 g/4 oz) black olives (preferably kalamata)

PROVENCAL DRESSING

1 tablespoon Dijon mustard

1 clove garlic, crushed

2 tablespoons tarragon or *wine vinegar*

1 tablespoon lemon juice, to taste

salt and freshly ground pepper

½ cup (125 mL/4 fl oz) extra virgin olive oil

1 tablespoon chopped herbs such as parsley, chives, oregano

PREHEAT the oven to 150°C (300°F). Put the tuna into an ovenproof pan in which it just fits snugly. Cover completely with the light olive oil and sprinkle the lemony herbs over the top. Cover well and bake in the oven for about 30 minutes. Remove and leave to cool in the oil. Boil the unpeeled new potatoes in salted water until tender. Do not allow to break. Drain.

LOWER the eggs carefully into warm water and bring the water slowly to the boil, stirring all the time so as to centre the yolks. Once the water is simmering, allow to cook for 8 minutes. Drain, lightly crack the eggshells and leave to cool completely in cold water. Drop the prepared beans into a little boiling salted water and cook until tender crisp. Drain immediately and refresh under cold water. Drain. Take out the tuna and drain. Cut into large chunks. Arrange the lettuce leaves on 4 large dinner plates or the base of a serving platter. Slice the potatoes thickly and arrange on top of the leaves. Shell the eggs and slice into quarters lengthwise. Arrange the beans, tomatoes, olives and eggs around the dishes or platter. Top with slices of tuna. Drizzle the dressing over the salad. If serving from a large serving platter, take a good wedge from it, ensuring that each person has a taste of everything.

TO MAKE the Provençal dressing, mix together the mustard, garlic, vinegar, lemon juice and salt and pepper to taste. Gradually beat in the olive oil—you need to do this slowly to ensure dressing remains thick and amalgamated. Beat again before using, adding herbs last of all.

FOOD PROCESSOR ALTERNATIVE

Add the mustard and garlic. Pour in the vinegar and lemon juice, and add the oil in a slow, steady stream with the motor running. Add the herbs last. Season to taste with salt and pepper.

SERVES 4

GARLIC CROUTONS may be added to this salad, people seem to enjoy the crunch. Cut 3 slices of good *levain* or white bread, remove crusts and cut into dice. Heat 2 tablespoons olive oil in a frying pan with 1 clove garlic. Add the bread and fry until golden. Drain on crumpled absorbent paper towels, and dust with a little salt.

TUNA

I sometimes use a good-quality canned tuna in olive oil (the best bears the name 'ventresco' on the label, which indicates that it is cut from the belly and is the most delicate part), or you can cook the fresh tuna yourself in olive oil. Tuna is readily available fresh at most fish markets; I like to purchase a sushi cut which is considered the top quality.

SMOKED SALMON SALAD

Crisp, juicy apples and tender celery are cut into julienne, giving texture and lightness to the delicate smoked salmon in creamy horseradish dressing. Top with a mound of golden fresh salmon eggs when these are available.

INGREDIENTS

250 g (8 oz) smoked salmon, sliced
2 crisp dessert apples such as Pink Lady or Fuji
4–5 tender stalks celery

DRESSING

½ cup (125 mL/4 fl oz) mayonnaise
2 tablespoons sour cream
2 teaspoons white wine vinegar

TO SERVE

2 tablespoons fresh salmon eggs (optional)
mesclun or other salad greens
extra virgin olive oil and balsamic vinegar

REMOVE 4 slices of salmon and reserve for garnish; cut the remaining salmon into strips. Cut the apple and celery into julienne. Put salmon, apple and celery into a bowl. Combine the dressing ingredients in a small bowl and fold lightly through the salad.

TO SERVE, pile the creamy salad in a mound on 4 dinner plates and top with a little mound of salmon eggs (if using). In a bowl, toss the mesclun or greens with a little olive oil and a dash of balsamic vinegar; pile beside the salmon. Roll the reserved salmon decoratively on the plate.

SERVES 4

GARDEN SALAD WITH ROASTED GOAT'S CHEESE CROUTES

There are many versions of the garden salad—the basic one uses whatever greens, flowers and herbs you may have in the garden or find at your greengrocers.

INGREDIENTS

a selection of greens such as curly
*   endive, radicchio, oakleaf lettuce,*
*   baby spinach leaves, watercress*
2 teaspoons balsamic vinegar
salt and freshly ground pepper
3 tablespoons each walnut or
*   hazelnut oil and virgin olive oil*
small handful of fresh chervil leaves
*   mixed with either sage flowers,*
*   nasturtium flowers, calendula*
*   petals or violets*
Roasted Goat's Cheese Croûtes
*   (recipe follows)*

PICK over the greens, removing any stems and browned leaves, and dry the leaves thoroughly. Wrap in a tea towel and place in the refrigerator to crisp until ready to serve. Whisk the balsamic vinegar, salt and pepper and oils in a bowl large enough to fit the salad greens. Put the greens and chervil with the flowers in the bowl with the dressing and toss gently but thoroughly. Pile little mounds of salad greens on large dinner plates, place 1 or 2 warm goat's cheese croûtes on each plate. Serves 4 for a light meal; 8 for a first course.

SERVES 4

ROASTED GOAT'S CHEESE CROUTES

Crisp bread rounds with a faint smear of garlic and goat's cheese are roasted. They make a nibble for drinks, a crisp addition to a salad and are delicious with a soup. Preheat the oven to 200°C (400°F). Butter or brush 8 thin slices of sourdough or French ficelle bread with olive oil. Rub a cut garlic clove over the bread slices and place a slice of fresh goat's cheese on each slice. Top with a sprig of thyme or oregano, drizzle on a little olive oil. Season with a good grinding of pepper and some sea salt. Arrange on a baking sheet. Bake in the oven for 10 minutes. Serve warm.

SALAD MIXTURES

An alternative is to buy fresh mesclun, which is a mixture of special leaves prepared by some growers or by the greengrocers themselves. Or you could use just one or two greens, such as watercress, baby spinach leaves or a soft-leaf lettuce such as butterhead or mignonette.

RIGHT: Garden Salad with Roasted Goat's Cheese Croûtes. Serve as a salad or offer the croûtes as a nibble with drinks

CHAPTER 3

VEGETABLE SPECIALS

A love of vegetables is almost a passport to good health. Now that growers are cultivating such a variety of vegetables—picking them much younger and smaller, and rushing them off to the markets—enthusiastic cooks are taking great delight in giving vegetables the star treatment.

BROAD BEANS WITH PANCETTA

Broad beans are a delightful luxury when they are young enough to be cooked whole, just topped and tailed, or eaten raw, as they love to do in France and Italy, accompanied with bread, cheese and a glass of wine. This dish can be served as a side dish with meat or tossed through pasta to make a delicious healthy meal.

INGREDIENTS

500 g (1 lb) fresh broad (fava) beans, unshelled
3 tablespoons extra virgin olive oil
1 small onion, finely chopped
125 g (4 oz) pancetta, cut into strips
salt and freshly ground black pepper, to taste

SHELL the beans, discarding the pods, and wash in cold water. In a saucepan of salted, boiling water, cook the beans for 8 minutes or until tender. Drain and remove the skins from the beans.

HEAT the oil in a large saucepan and sauté the onion until soft. Add the pancetta strips and cook for 2–3 minutes. Add the beans and a good grinding of pepper, tossing. Cook over a gentle heat for 1 minute, season with salt and serve at once.

SERVES 4

PANCETTA

Pancetta, air-dried pork belly, is the Italian answer to bacon or speck. Each have their own distinctive flavours and can be used in this recipe. For a delicate flavour, cover the strips of pancetta with water, bring to the boil then drain, discarding the water. Proceed with the recipe.

CHIVE AND RICOTTA-STUFFED ZUCCHINI FLOWERS

Zucchini flowers are available in summer and autumn, sometimes with zucchini attached.

INGREDIENTS

12 zucchini (courgette) flowers or
  500 g (1 lb) baby zucchini with
  flowers still attached
250 g (8 oz) fresh ricotta cheese
a grating of nutmeg
1 bunch fresh chives, snipped
1 egg, beaten
4 tablespoons grated Parmesan
  cheese
salt and freshly ground black pepper
light olive oil, for frying

BATTER

2 eggs
½ cup (60 g/2 oz) plain (all-purpose)
  flour
½ cup (125 mL/4 fl oz) soda water

BEGIN by making the batter. Beat the eggs in a shallow bowl, whisk in the flour with a fork and add the soda water to make a smooth consistency. The batter should not be too thick; the excess should drain off quickly. Set aside.

WASH the flowers or zucchini gently and dry well with a kitchen cloth. In a small bowl, mix the ricotta with the nutmeg, chives, beaten egg, Parmesan cheese and salt and pepper to taste. Carefully open the flowers and spoon the ricotta filling in each. Squeeze gently in the palm of the hand to enclose filling thoroughly.

TO COOK, heat about 5–6 cm (2 in.) of light olive oil in a pan or wok. Dip the flowers or zucchini with stuffed flowers into the batter, draining off excess, and fry a few at a time until golden brown. Drain on absorbent paper towels for a moment, then serve.

SERVES 4–6

PAN-FRIED CHERRY TOMATOES

Serve this as a fresh-tasting vegetable side dish, or toss the tomatoes through cooked pasta.

INGREDIENTS

24–30 cherry tomatoes, depending
  on size, washed and stemmed
2 tablespoons light olive oil
1 clove garlic, chopped
1 tablespoon freshly chopped parsley
6 fresh basil leaves, slivered
salt and freshly ground black pepper

HEAT the oil in a frying pan, add the tomatoes, garlic and parsley, and cook the mixture over a moderate heat for about 2–3 minutes, or until tomatoes are heated through. Take care not to allow the skins to split. Just before serving, toss in the slivered basil and season with salt and pepper to taste.

SERVES 4–6

BRAISED ARTICHOKES WITH HERBED STUFFING

The leafy bud of a plant of the thistle family, the artichoke is one of our most elegant and much loved vegetables.

INGREDIENTS

6–8 young globe artichokes

1 cup (60 g/2 oz) soft breadcrumbs

½ cup (60g/2 oz) grated Parmesan cheese

3 tablespoons chopped herbs such as parsley, oregano, mint

salt and freshly ground pepper

3 tablespoons olive oil

1 onion, peeled and chopped

To TRIM ARTICHOKES

Remove outer leaves, then cut one-third off the top of the artichoke with a sharp knife. Trim the stalk with scissors, leaving 5 cm (2 in.) of stalk. As each one is prepared, rub the surface with a sliced lemon.

TRIM and prepare artichokes (see hint). Make a stuffing by combining the breadcrumbs, Parmesan cheese, herbs and salt and pepper to taste. Moisten with 1 tablespoon olive oil. Open the leaves of the artichokes slightly and fill the spaces with the stuffing. Drizzle in a little extra oil.

STAND the artichokes upright in an oiled flameproof casserole or heavy saucepan. Pour in a little water and the remaining 2 tablespoons olive oil; add the chopped onion. Cover and cook over a low heat for 40 minutes, basting from time to time with the juices. To serve, arrange artichokes with their stalks in the air, and spoon over some of the juices.

SERVES 6

NOTE To eat, lift off a leaf and scrape the fleshy base between the teeth. As you reach the heart, remove the fibrous 'choke' if there, then enjoy the delicious base.

SUGAR-FRIED SWEET POTATOES

INGREDIENTS

750 g (1½ lb) sweet potatoes, yams or kumera

30 g (1 oz) butter

½ cup (90 g/3 oz) soft brown sugar

LEFT: Braised Artichokes with Herbed Stuffing is a spectacular first course

IN A medium saucepan, boil the sweet potatoes in water until almost cooked. Drain, peel and cut into quarters lengthwise; if long, cut in two. Melt the butter in a frying pan. Add the potatoes and sprinkle with the sugar, stirring with the butter to form a kind of caramel. Turn the potatoes frequently in order to coat evenly, forming a very crunchy crust, about 5–7 minutes.

SERVES 4

ROASTED TOMATOES WITH SHALLOTS

An elegant first course which relies on flavoursome red Roma (plum) tomatoes and delicious little golden shallots, both roasted.

INGREDIENTS

12 golden shallots, peeled

about 8 tablespoons virgin olive oil

2 teaspoons caster (superfine) sugar

12 ripe red Roma (plum) tomatoes

1 tablespoon balsamic or *wine vinegar*

sea salt and freshly ground pepper

fresh basil leaves, to garnish

PEELING GOLDEN SHALLOTS

To peel shallots, first place in a bowl. Pour over boiling water. Let stand for 1 minute, then drain and refresh under cold water before peeling.

PREHEAT the oven to 200°C (400°F). Arrange the shallots on a sheet of foil, sprinkle with 2 tablespoons olive oil and the caster sugar. Fold up the sides of the foil and seal the edges to make an airtight parcel. Bake in the oven for 45 minutes. Meanwhile, halve the tomatoes, drizzle with 2 tablespoons olive oil and roast in the same oven for 20 minutes.

ADD the vinegar to a small bowl with sea salt and pepper to taste and gradually whisk in the remaining 4 tablespoons olive oil until a thickened dressing is formed. Whisk in the juices from the tomatoes. Arrange the roasted tomatoes on a salad platter and spoon around the dressing. Top each tomato half with a shallot (halved, if large) and garnish with shredded basil leaves.

SERVES 4–6

SILVERBEET WITH SULTANAS AND PINE NUTS

Sweet sultanas and toasted pine nuts add interest to silverbeet.

INGREDIENTS

1 bunch silverbeet

2 tablespoons unsalted butter

2 tablespoons olive oil

1 clove garlic, finely chopped

½ teaspoon salt

¼ cup (30 g/1 oz) pine nuts, toasted

⅓ cup (60 g/2 oz) sultanas

REMOVE the stalks from the silverbeet, wash and shake dry. Stack the leaves and cut into thin strips. In a large frying pan, heat the butter and oil, and add the garlic and salt. Add the silverbeet and sauté over a moderate heat for about 3–5 minutes or until tender. Add the pine nuts and sultanas, and toss to combine. Serve.

SERVES 4

WOOD MUSHROOM NICOISE

It is fascinating to find such an assortment of mushrooms these days. Take advantage of them—they each have their own texture, shape and flavour.

INGREDIENTS

750 g (1½ lb) assorted fresh
  mushrooms—button, shiitake,
  Swiss brown, slippery jack
¼ cup (60 mL/2 fl oz) olive oil
2 cloves garlic, peeled and crushed
1 bay leaf
2 tomatoes, skinned, seeded and
  chopped, or 12 tiny toms, whole
salt and freshly ground pepper
10–12 small black olives
2 tablespoons chopped fresh parsley

WITH a damp cloth, wipe away any dirt from the mushrooms or use a soft brush to remove grass. Handle gently. Quarter the mushrooms, if large, keeping both caps and stems. Heat the oil in a flameproof casserole with the garlic and bay leaf.

WHEN the oil is hot, add the mushrooms. Cook over a high heat for 5 minutes, stirring constantly. Add the chopped tomatoes or whole tiny tomatoes. Season to taste with salt and pepper. Bring to the simmer. Add olives and cook, covered, for a further 5 minutes. Top with parsley (or chervil if you have it). Serve warm or cold in little dishes, with crusty bread to mop up the juices.

SERVES 6

PARSNIP PUREE WITH PEAS

The nutty flavour of parsnips makes a fabulous vegetable purée, mellowed by the potato. Serve with grilled or roasted poultry or meats

INGREDIENTS

500 g (1 lb) parsnips, peeled and cut
  into chunky pieces
1 large potato, peeled and quartered
½ teaspoon salt
1 cup (185 g/6 oz) shelled green
  peas, fresh or frozen
2 spring onions (scallions), chopped
30 g (1 oz) unsalted butter, cut into
  pieces and softened
3 tablespoons milk
salt and freshly ground pepper

ADD the parsnips and potato to a large, heavy saucepan of cold water. Bring the water to the boil, then add the salt. Boil for 8–10 minutes or until tender. Meanwhile, cook the peas in a small saucepan of boiling water until tender. Drain and transfer to a bowl of iced water. In a bowl, add the spring onions, butter, milk and drained peas. Drain the parsnips and potato, return to the pan and steam over a moderate heat, stirring for about 1 minute, to evaporate any excess liquid. Purée the parsnip mixture, season to taste with salt and pepper, and add to the bowl of peas. Fold the mixture lightly to combine.

SERVES 4

GRILLED VEGETABLES WITH SAGE AND GARLIC MAYONNAISE

*A wonderful start to a relaxed meal, each guest makes a selection
of vegetables to dip in the unctuous mayonnaise.*

INGREDIENTS

½ cup (125mL/4 fl oz) olive oil

2 cloves garlic, chopped

¼ cup (60 mL/2 fl oz) rice vinegar

2 leeks, washed and halved

2 small zucchini (courgettes), peeled
  and quartered lengthwise

4 button squash, halved

4 baby eggplants (aubergines),
  halved lengthwise

1 red onion, quartered lengthwise

1 head young garlic, halved
  crosswise

1 red or yellow capsicum (sweet
  pepper), trimmed and cut into its
  natural lobes, seeds discarded

1 bunch fresh asparagus, tough stalk
  ends snapped off

3 large green or red chillies

SAGE AND GARLIC MAYONNAISE

1 cup (250 mL/8 fl oz) homemade
  mayonnaise (page 12)

1½ tablespoons rice vinegar

1 tablespoon tamari or soy sauce

juice of ½ lemon

2 tablespoons white sesame seeds,
  toasted

1 small red chilli, finely chopped

2 cloves garlic, finely chopped

1½ tablespoons Dijon mustard

8 fresh sage leaves, finely chopped

IN A large bowl, whisk together the oil, garlic and rice vinegar. Add the zucchini, squash, eggplant, red onion, garlic, capsicum, asparagus and chillies. Toss gently. Marinate at room temperature for 1 hour. When ready to cook, remove vegetables from marinade and arrange them on the grill over medium-hot coals or on a preheated ribbed grill. You can cook them under a domestic griller (broiler). Cook until tender, about 4 minutes on each side. Serve the Sage and Garlic Mayonnaise on the side.

SERVES 4

SAGE AND GARLIC MAYONNAISE

Spoon the homemade mayonnaise into a bowl. Stir in the vinegar, tamari or soy sauce, lemon juice, sesame seeds, chilli, garlic, mustard and chopped sage. Cover and chill until ready to serve.

VEGETABLES

*Tender young vegetables are an inspiration for any cook. I like to make
a platter of colourful vegetables lightly grilled and serve them with good
mayonnaise with an Asian influence. Most tender young vegetables can
be cooked this way—mushrooms, potato, sweet potato or yam slices,
or halved tomatoes.*

RIGHT: Grilled Vegetables with Sage and Garlic Mayonnaise is very much a dish that fits in with today's casual way of eating

BAKED EGGPLANT
WITH BASIL PESTO

*Slice halved eggplant (aubergine) almost through like the pages of a book, and
fill with delicious Mediterranean herb paste, then tomatoes and cheese.*

INGREDIENTS

*4 small or 2 medium eggplants
(aubergines)*

*about 2 tablespoons of pesto
(page 49)*

2–3 vine-ripened tomatoes, sliced

*1 small mozzarella cheese, sliced
thinly*

1 tablespoon olive oil

2 tablespoons water

PREHEAT the oven to 180°C (350°F). Wash the eggplants and
halve lengthwise. Place cut edge down on a chopping board, then slice
the flesh lengthwise in 4 or 5 places, not cutting through to flat surface.
Spread the pesto over the cut surfaces of the eggplant and insert slices
of tomato and mozzarella into the cuts. Place the eggplants in an oiled
ovenproof dish, drizzle over the oil. Add 2 tablespoons water to the
dish and cover—foil may be used. Cook in the oven for 30–45 minutes
or until eggplants are cooked. Set aside to cool and serve warm with
crusty bread.

SERVES 4

JULIENNE OF ZUCCHINI
WITH PISTACHIO PESTO

*Zucchini (courgettes) have a light delicate flavour when cooked and take on a
new dimension with this flavour-packed sauce.*

INGREDIENTS

30 g (1 oz) unsalted butter

*750 g (1½ lb) zucchini (courgettes),
cut into matchsticks*

Pistachio Pesto (page 49)

ZUCCHINI are easy to cut into matchsticks, simply use a hand
mandolin or vegetable cutter fitted with a julienne blade. Melt butter
and sauté the zucchini for 3–4 minutes, or until crisp-tender. Add the
pesto and quickly toss to heat through. Serve immediately.

SERVES 6

BASIL PESTO

A marvellous sauce with many uses, it is sublime folded through cooked hot spaghetti. Add it to potato gnocchi, enjoy it on bruschetta, add a few dots to pizza, spoon over boiled new potatoes or toss through steamed vegetables.

INGREDIENTS

2 cups fresh basil leaves

2 tablespoons chopped pine nuts

2 cloves garlic, peeled and crushed

pinch of coarse salt

¼ cup (30 g/1 oz) grated Parmesan cheese

½ cup (125 mL/4 fl oz) extra virgin olive oil

COMBINE the basil, pine nuts, garlic and salt. Grind in a food processor or electric blender (done in several lots) or with a pestle, crushing the ingredients to form a paste. Add the Parmesan cheese and grind again until the mixture is blended. Add the olive oil in a thin stream, whisking constantly, to make a mayonnaise consistency. Store in a clean, airtight jar in the refrigerator.

MAKES ABOUT 1 CUP

PISTACHIO PESTO Make as above, using pistachio nuts in place of the pine nuts.

ROASTED VEGETABLE SALAD

This delicious warm dish of colourful vegetables is made using vegetables in season. Asparagus, baby button squash or zucchini (courgette) may be used.

INGREDIENTS

500 g (1 lb) baby finger-length eggplants (aubergine)

1 bunch large spring onions (scallions) or baby leeks, peeled and trimmed

2 red capsicum (sweet peppers), quartered and seeds removed

1 bulb garlic, broken into cloves

1 kg (2 lb) vine-ripened tomatoes, whole or halved

½ cup (125 mL/4 fl oz) olive oil

sea salt

chopped flat-leaf (Italian) parsley, to garnish

PREHEAT the oven to 180°C (350°F). In a heavy baking dish, drizzle the vegetables with half the olive oil and roast until very soft, about 35–40 minutes. Cover tightly with a lid or foil, and leave for 10 minutes or so. Uncover and skin the peppers, if liked. If the eggplants are baby ones, leave unpeeled and whole; leave the onions whole. While still warm, dress the vegetables with the remaining olive oil and season with salt. Turn into a serving dish and scatter with the parsley. Serve while still warm.

SERVES 4–6

REMOVING SKINS OF PISTACHIO NUTS

Parboil 3 tablespoons shelled pistachio nuts for 2 minutes, then slip skins off or rub briskly between absorbent paper towels.

BABY BOK CHOY WITH OYSTER SAUCE

This dish looks so attractive, with the vivid green of the bok choy, the dark, earthy brown shades of the shiitake mushrooms and the creamy, elegant oyster mushrooms. It is also delicious, and light yet filling. Look for bok choy, shiitake mushrooms and oyster at oriental food stores or good greengrocers; many have the fresh mushrooms. Growers are now supplying baby bok choy—some only finger length in size—they are exquisite when cooked and look like precious jade.

INGREDIENTS

500 g (1 lb) baby bok choy
125 g (4 oz) shiitake mushrooms
125 g (4 oz) oyster mushrooms
4 cloves garlic, chopped
1 tablespoon finely grated ginger
2 tablespoons vegetable oil
1 teaspoon sesame oil
1 teaspoon soy sauce
2 teaspoons rice wine vinegar
½ teaspoon cornflour (cornstarch)
1 tablespoon oyster sauce

CUT the bases off the bok choy. Baby bok choy may be left whole. If the bok choy is large, trim the base and halve or quarter the vegetable; trim the rough tops of the leaves, but keep plenty of stalk on each leaf. Wash and dry the leaves, and cut each across into 2 or 3 pieces. Trim the stalks of the mushrooms; slash a cross or star on the rounded side of the shiitake mushrooms.

HEAT the vegetable and sesame oils in a wok or large frying pan over a medium heat and stir-fry the mushrooms. Cook the mushrooms until they give up some juice and then reabsorb it. Add the garlic and ginger, and stir-fry for 1 minute. Add the bok choy and continue to stir-fry until wilted, about 1 minute. Have ready the soy sauce, vinegar, cornflour and oyster sauce combined in a small bowl. Add this mixture to the vegetables and cook for about 1 minute, or until the vegetables are glazed. Serve immediately in a warmed serving dish.

SERVES 4

DRIED SHIITAKE MUSHROOMS

Shiitake mushrooms can often be bought dried from Chinese or oriental grocery sections in most delicatessens or supermarkets. To reconstitute, cover with boiling water and soak for 20 minutes. Trim stems and use as instructed in the recipe.

RIGHT: Baby Bok Choy with Oyster Sauce makes a fast, but tempting dish for a light lunch, a starter or to serve with other Chinese dishes

POTATOES DAUPHINOISE GRATIN

This gratin of potatoes is one of the best and most useful dishes to have in your repertoire. Thin slices of potato are cooked in creamy milk—sometimes egg is beaten in to make it richer and sometimes a little cheese such as Gruyère is added. It is a wonderful accompaniment to a large joint such as roast beef or roasted chicken.

INGREDIENTS

7 medium-sized potatoes, old or
yellow flesh
salt and freshly ground pepper
grated nutmeg
1 cup (125 g/4 oz) grated Gruyère
cheese (optional)
1 clove garlic, peeled
1½ cups (375 mL/12 fl oz) milk or
half milk and fresh (single, light)
cream
30 g (1 oz) butter, cut into pieces

COOKING FOR A CROWD

When cooking for a crowd
(8–10 people), use 8–10 potatoes.
Slicing them is easy in a food
processor fitted with a slicing
attachment. As the cooking may
take 2 hours, you can cook the dish
first in a microwave on medium for
1 hour, then transfer it to the oven
for 30–40 minutes—convenient if
oven space is at a premium.

PREHEAT the oven to 190°C (375°F). Peel and slice the potatoes thinly. Butter a shallow gratin dish. Arrange a layer of potato slices, sprinkle with salt, pepper and nutmeg. Repeat layers until all potatoes are used. If using Gruyère cheese, strew over each layer.

MASH the clove of garlic, add to the milk, or milk and cream, in a saucepan. Heat the milk, but do not boil, and pour over the potatoes. Dot with the butter and cover loosely with foil. Bake in the oven for about 1½ hours. Check after 1½ hours; if the liquid has not been absorbed, remove the foil. The potatoes should be browned on the top and creamy moist within. Serve hot from the dish.

SERVES 6

POTATOES BOULANGERE This gratin of potatoes is cooked as for dauphinoise, with 2 sliced onions replacing the cheese and beef stock replacing the milk.

STOVIES This is the Scottish version of gratin potatoes. Layer sliced potatoes with sliced onions in a gratin dish. Add tiny bits of butter or good beef dripping here and there, and season with salt and pepper. Cover with beef stock and cook as above. Bacon stovies use bacon fat in place of the butter or beef dripping.

POTATOES SAVOYARD This gratin of potatoes is cooked as for dauphinoise, but with the addition of bacon and fresh chives. Take 4–6 bacon rashers, trim off the rind and fry or grill until crisp. Cut into pieces and add with 2 tablespoons snipped chives between the layers of potato.

CRUSTY GARLIC AND ROSEMARY POTATOES

This is a very Italian way with potatoes, cooked in olive oil with garlic and fresh rosemary.

INGREDIENTS

500 g (1 lb) small red or new
  potatoes, quartered
3 cloves garlic, peeled and sliced
1 tablespoon olive oil
1 teaspoon rosemary spikes
salt and freshly ground black
  pepper, to taste

IN A saucepan, steam the potatoes, covered, for 8–10 minutes or until just tender. In a heavy frying pan, cook the garlic in the oil over a moderate heat, stirring, until pale gold. Add the potatoes and rosemary, and season with salt and pepper to taste. Sauté the potatoes over a moderate to high heat, stirring, for 5 minutes or until the potatoes are golden and fragrant with garlic and rosemary.

SERVES 2–4

POTATOES ANNA

I like to make this classic French golden potato cake in a solid cast-iron frying pan which can be put in the oven. Alternatively, a cake pan can be used.

INGREDIENTS

1 kg (2 lb) old potatoes, medium
  size and uniform shape
60 g (2 oz) butter
salt

POTATOES

Do not buy any variety of potato that has green skin or flesh. Potatoes should feel very firm and have a faint earthy smell. Store the potatoes in a cool, dark place. They keep particularly well if they are left unwashed, with earth still clinging to the skins. Buy new potatoes in small quantities because they do not keep well.

PREHEAT the oven to 200°C (400°F). Peel the potatoes and, using a mandolin or a very sharp knife, cut into wafer-thin slices. Place in a colander and wash well under cold, running water. Dry well in a kitchen cloth and place in a large bowl.

MELT the butter and toss in the potatoes with a large pinch of salt. Line a thick, heavy frying pan, about 18 cm (7 in.) diameter, with potato slices in neat overlapping circles. Continue filling pan in even circles with remaining potatoes.

PLACE over a gentle heat and brown lightly. Use a metal spatula or knife to lift and check the potatoes are not burning. When a good colour underneath, place in the oven for 30 minutes or until potatoes are tender and golden. Place a heated serving plate on top of pan and flip over to turn out potatoes. Serve very hot.

SERVES 4–6

CHAPTER 4

TIME FOR LUNCH

When lunch time approaches, the question of whether you will enjoy a light, fresh-tasting soup or a simple salad, a frittata or a delicious creamy risotto with wonderful Arborio rice arises. You may invite friends over to share warm, fragrant bread or a leek and tomato tarte tatin, straight from the oven, and a glass of crisp wine. Planning a delicious lunch is one of the great pleasures of cooking.

TORTONI WITH OLIVES

A great Italian bread filled with pine nuts and olives.
Serve in wedges—perfect for a picnic, an alfresco lunch in the garden or
by the fireside in winter.

INGREDIENTS

30 g (1 oz) fresh yeast or
  1½ teaspoons dried yeast
3½ cups (435 g/14 oz) plain
  (all-purpose) flour
2 teaspoons white granulated sugar
2 tablespoons warm water, plus
  1½ cups (375 mL/12 fl oz) extra
½ cup (125 g/4 oz) fine yellow
  cornmeal
½ teaspoon salt
5 tablespoons olive oil, plus extra
  for greasing
1 egg, beaten
Pine Nut and Olive Filling
  (page 56)

LEFT: Tortoni with Olives, a superb bread baked with a mixture of black olives, garlic, herbs and pine nuts

BREAK up the yeast and blend lightly with a little of the flour, the sugar and 2 tablespoons warm water; leave for 10–15 minutes. Mix together the remaining flour, cornmeal, yeast mixture and salt in a bowl, and make a well in the centre. Add the extra warm water and bring the dough together. Knead on a floured surface for 10 minutes, until smooth and elastic. Roll out the dough and brush with 1 tablespoon olive oil. Fold over the dough and knead in the oil. Repeat with the remaining oil. Place in a greased bowl and sprinkle with a few drops of water. Cover the bowl and leave in a warm place for an 1 hour to double in size.

KNEAD the dough for 1 minute and divide into two. Roll out two rounds 25 cm (10 in.) in diameter. Put one round on a greased and floured baking sheet. Place Pine Nut and Olive Filling in the middle and spread out, not quite to the edge. Dampen the edges with water and place the second round on top. Seal edges then brush the loaf with the beaten egg. Cover with plastic wrap and leave in a warm place for 20 minutes. Prick top with a fork. Meanwhile, preheat the oven to 200°C (400°F). Bake the loaf for about 20 minutes, until golden brown. Serve warm or cold, cut in wedges.

SERVES 8

INGREDIENTS

2 tablespoons olive oil

1 small onion, chopped

1 clove garlic, crushed

*¾ cup (125 g/4 oz) pitted black
    olives, halved*

salt and freshly ground pepper

½ cup (75 g/2½ oz) pine nuts

1 teaspoon chopped fresh thyme

4 teaspoons chopped fresh parsley

PINE NUT AND OLIVE FILLING

Heat the oil and gently cook the onion and garlic for 8–10 minutes,
or until softened. Add the remaining ingredients, cook for a further
2 minutes and set aside to cool until needed.

FRESH BREAD

*Freshly made bread keeps best if loosely covered with a clean napkin or
cloth, and left to cool.*

ONIONS STUFFED
TUSCAN STYLE

*In France and Italy, stuffed vegetables are often served as an entrée.
When their stuffing is seasoned with fresh herbs and Parmesan cheese,
onions become an interesting dish.*

INGREDIENTS

6 large onions, peeled, left whole

30 g (1 oz) butter

*2 rashers (slices) bacon, rind
    removed and diced*

*250 g (8 oz) lean steak mince
    (ground beef)*

1 spring onion (scallion), chopped

1 tablespoon snipped chives

2 tablespoons chopped parsley

*¾ cup (45 g/1½ oz) fresh
    breadcrumbs*

*4 tablespoons freshly grated
    Parmesan cheese*

salt and freshly ground pepper

2 tablespoons extra virgin olive oil

*1 cup (250 mL/8 fl oz) chicken
    stock*

PREHEAT the oven to 200°C (400°F). Place the onions in a
saucepan and cover with salted water. Cover pan with lid. Bring to the
boil, reduce heat and simmer for 10 minutes. Drain.

CAREFULLY peel the onions, cutting the top and bottom off each,
and scoop out the centre from the inside, leaving a thick shell. Finely
dice the centres. Melt the butter in a heavy frying pan and sauté the
diced onion until softened. Add the bacon and cook for a further
2 minutes. Add the steak mince, spring onion, chives, parsley,
breadcrumbs, Parmesan cheese and salt and pepper to taste. Stir
thoroughly. Spoon the stuffing into the onion shells. Place in a greased
shallow baking dish and drizzle over the olive oil. Pour the stock
around the onions and bake in the oven for 35–45 minutes, or until
tender and golden brown.

SERVES 6

RISOTTO MILANESE

Risotto is a speciality dish of northern Italy where it is much appreciated—for it is a dish that must have the cook's full attention. The best risotto is made from Arborio rice, a small, round grain which is capable of absorbing a great amount of liquid without disintegrating.

INGREDIENTS

8 cups (2 litres/3¼ imp. pints)
  chicken stock
good pinch (about ½ teaspoon) of
  saffron threads
90 g (3 oz) butter
1 small onion, finely chopped
1¾ cups (370 g/13 oz) Arborio rice,
  unwashed
½ cup (125 mL/4 fl oz) dry white
  wine
½ cup (60 g/2 oz) grated Parmesan
  cheese
salt and freshly ground black pepper

COOKING RISOTTO

This method of cooking risotto results in a creamy rice with each grain separate and still firm to the bite. The liquid is added slowly and stirred constantly, and must be absorbed after each addition before more is added. Use a heavy saucepan, preferably with a rounded bottom to prevent the rice sticking. It needs to be big enough to accommodate the rice, which will swell as much as three times when cooked. The stock for adding must be kept simmering next to the risotto pan, to prevent slowing down of the cooking process.

BRING the chicken stock to a simmer and keep hot. Put the saffron in a small bowl, add 4 tablespoons simmering stock and set aside. In a heavy saucepan, melt half the butter, add the onion and cook gently, stirring until softened. Add the rice and stir for 3–4 minutes. Stir in the wine and, when evaporated, add a ladle of the simmering stock. Cook over a moderate heat, stirring until the stock is absorbed. Add the remaining stock a ladle at a time, ensuring stock is absorbed before each addition and stirring constantly. Lastly, add the saffron-steeped stock. The rice should be cooked after 20 minutes. At this stage, remove the pan from the heat and, without stirring, allow the rice to absorb the last of the liquid. Just before serving, fold in the remaining butter and the Parmesan; stir well into the rice. Season to taste.

SERVES 4

MUSHROOM RISOTTO Slice 250 g (8 oz) button mushrooms or wild or wood mushrooms (cêpes, fly caps, slippery jacks or Swiss browns). Heat 1 tablespoon butter and 2 tablespoons olive oil in a frying pan, add the mushrooms and toss over a high heat for 1–2 minutes. Prepare the risotto as above (without the saffron), adding half the mushrooms with the last of the stock. Add the remaining mushrooms with the Parmesan. For a richer flavour when you can't find wild mushrooms, soak 30 g (1 oz) imported dried wild mushrooms—porcini or cêpes—in ½ cup (125 mL/4 fl oz) hot stock; let sit for 30 minutes. Drain, chop the mushrooms and sauté with onions; add the mushroom stock to the hot stock.

ASPARAGUS RISOTTO Cut off the tough ends of 10 spears fresh asparagus. Remove tips and reserve; slice the remaining spears. Prepare the risotto as above (without the saffron), adding the sliced asparagus along with the onion. The tips are added after the last of the stock and will steam in the liquid as it being absorbed into the rice.

RISOTTO WITH GREEN PEAS Shell enough fresh young peas to make 1 cup peas. Make the risotto as above (with or without the saffron) and add the peas with the last addition of stock.

PENNE WITH ROCKET, TOMATOES AND PARMESAN

*Rocket, also known as arugula, makes a pungent, peppery sauce for pasta.
Here it is cooked until just wilted with tomatoes in a hot, peppery oil.*

INGREDIENTS

*250 g (8 oz) penne or other chunky
pasta*

3 large cloves garlic, thinly sliced

*1 red bird's eye chilli, seeded and
chopped*

4 tablespoons olive oil

*1 bunch rocket (arugula), washed
thoroughly, trimmed and coarsely
chopped*

*4 ripe Roma (plum) tomatoes,
halved, seeded and chopped*

*freshly shaved Parmigiano-Reggiano
cheese*

COOK the pasta in a large saucepan of boiling, salted water until al dente, about 8–10 minutes. Meanwhile, lightly sauté the garlic and chilli in 2 tablespoons oil, about 2 minutes, on no account letting it brown which will render the dish bitter. Add the rocket and tomatoes, and continue cooking, tossing all the time until the greens are wilted and the tomatoes heated through.

DRAIN the pasta thoroughly, add the rocket mixture and toss to combine well. Scoop into bowls to serve, drizzle with the remaining oil and top with shaved Parmigiano-Reggiano.

SERVES 4

PARMESAN CHEESE

*Parmigiano-Reggiano is the best Parmesan cheese and will have its name
clearly stamped on the crust. There are strict laws guiding the
manufacturing techniques of the cheese. It is produced from cow's milk
between April and November, and comes only from the Italian provinces
of Parma, Reggio-Emilia, Modena (which is also where good balsamic
vinegar comes from), Bologna and Mantova. Grana padano is cheaper, but
inferior cheese, being less matured and slightly damper in consistency.
Always buy Parmesan cheese by the piece and grate it freshly as you need
it. Store wrapped in a piece of calico and covered with foil, or in a hemp
bag (which should be kept damp) in the refrigerator.*

RIGHT: Penne with Rocket, Tomatoes and Parmesan is a lovely luncheon salad. Watercress sprigs can replace the rocket

FRESH VEGETABLE LASAGNE

The vegetables can be prepared beforehand and the pasta sheets made ready for cooking to make things easier when entertaining.

INGREDIENTS

6 Roma (plum) tomatoes, halved

2 tablespoons olive oil

1 each of red and yellow capsicum (sweet pepper)

1 small sweet potato (kumera)

1 medium eggplant (aubergine), thinly sliced lengthwise

2 zucchini (courgettes), thinly sliced lengthwise

extra virgin olive oil

12 lasagne sheets (page 125)

small bunch rocket (arugula) or spinach leaves, washed and stems removed

155 g (5 oz) fresh or baked ricotta, sliced

freshly cracked black pepper

GRILLING VEGETABLES

To grill vegetables, heat a domestic grill (broiler) and cook vegetables on the heated oiled grill plate. Alternatively, heat a ribbed grill, brush with oil and cook vegetables on the hot surface. Both ways give a good result.

PREHEAT the oven to 160°C (325°F). Arrange the halved tomatoes in a baking dish (roasting pan) and lightly drizzle over the olive oil. Bake in the oven for 1 hour. Remove the tomatoes and increase the oven to 180°C (350°F). Place the capsicums on an oiled baking sheet and grill (broil) under a high heat until the skin has blackened, turning frequently. Cool the capsicums in a paper bag then scrape off the blackened skin. Cut the flesh into pieces and set aside.

WASH the sweet potato, but do not peel it. Place it in a small saucepan of boiling, salted water and cook until barely soft, about 10 minutes. Drain, cool and peel. Slice the sweet potato and set aside.

PREHEAT a grill (broiler) or ribbed grill to hot and arrange the eggplant slices on an oiled grill plate. Brush with a little extra virgin olive oil and grill, under the hot grill or on ribbed grill, turning once, brushing with extra oil as they cook, until coloured and tender, about 10 minutes. Repeat the process with the sliced zucchini.

COOK the pasta in a large saucepan of boiling, salted water for 8–10 minutes until al dente. Remove carefully with a slotted spoon and drain.

PLACE four sheets of lasagne onto a large baking sheet, add a layer of rocket, then a slice of ricotta, sweet potato and eggplant slices, and roasted tomato halves. Add a second sheet of pasta to each, then the zucchini slices, roasted capsicums, more sweet potato and top with the final layer of pasta. Drizzle each with a little extra virgin olive oil and sprinkle over a little pepper. Cover with foil and bake in the oven for 10–15 minutes until thoroughly hot. Cut into thick, wide serves. Arrange a lasagne package on each plate and serve immediately. You may offer a very good olive oil to drizzle over the lasagne and a few fresh greens.

SERVES 4

WILD MUSHROOM PASTA

Wild mushrooms are not only found in our forests. Growers are supplying us with fresh Swiss browns, shiitake, oyster mushrooms and porcini. Or obtain the wild taste by soaking dried boletus or cêpes in water and combine with cultivated mushrooms.

INGREDIENTS

375 g (12 oz) wild mushrooms such
   as cêpes, slippery jacks or mixture
   of Swiss browns and shiitake
30 g (1 oz) dried cêpes or boletus
3 tablespoons olive oil
1 small red chilli, seeded and
   chopped
3 cloves garlic, chopped
½ cup (125 mL/4 fl oz) dry white
   wine
2–3 tablespoons chopped parsley
salt and freshly ground black pepper
375 g (12 oz) tagliatelle

WIPE the mushrooms with a damp cloth. Slice the mushrooms, removing any tough stems. Soak the dried mushrooms in just enough hot water to cover. Heat the oil and chilli in a medium saucepan, add the garlic and cook gently, but do not allow to brown. Add the sliced and dried soaked mushrooms with the soaking liquid. Cook over a high heat for 1–2 minutes, tossing continuously. Add the wine, reduce the heat and cook for 5–10 minutes. Add the parsley and season.

MEANWHILE, cook the pasta in a large saucepan of boiling, salted water until al dente. Drain the pasta, toss with the mushrooms and serve. Other pastas may be used, such as fettuccine or one of the shaped pastas like penne, oriechiette or green pasta.

SERVES 6

ITALIAN FRIED SANDWICHES

The kind of sandwich you might find at Harry's Bar in Venice at lunchtime, or in Paris you may see these offered as croques monsieur. *Serve with cornichons, those tiny French pickled gherkins.*

INGREDIENTS

2 teaspoons Dijon mustard
8 slices buttered white bread such as
   levain or sourdough
125 g (4 oz) cheddar or Gruyère
   cheese, sliced
12 slices ham or mortadella
2 eggs
1 tablespoon oil, plus a little extra
salt and freshly ground black pepper
oil, for shallow-frying

SPREAD the mustard evenly over the buttered side of the bread. Arrange the cheese on 4 slices and top with the ham or mortadella. Cover with remaining bread and press firmly together. Beat the eggs and oil together, adding salt and pepper to taste. Dip each sandwich into this mixture and let the bread absorb some of the egg. Heat the extra oil in a frying pan and fry 2 sandwiches at a time until golden brown, turning with an egg slice to crisp both sides. Drain on absorbent paper towels and serve.

SERVES 4

ROASTED VEGETABLE AND GOAT'S CHEESE PIZZA

A delicious pizza which all will like, vegetarians will give it a big tick. The goat's cheese can be replaced with milder tasting bocconcini or mozzarella.

INGREDIENTS

about 6 tablespoons olive oil

1 medium-size sweet potato (kumera), peeled and cut into thin slices

2 finger eggplants (aubergines), sliced into quarters lengthwise

2 small zucchini (courgettes), sliced into quarters lengthwise

1 red salad onion, cut into wedges (with roots attached)

100 g (3½ oz) goat's cheese or bocconcini or mozzarella, sliced

1 tablespoon pine nuts

1 tablespoon fresh oregano leaves

PIZZA BASE

2¼ cups (280 g/9 oz) plain (all-purpose) flour

1 teaspoon salt

1 sachet dried yeast

1 teaspoon sugar

¾ cup (185 mL/6 fl oz) lukewarm milk

1 large egg

60 g (2 oz) softened butter

PREPARE the pizza base (method follows) and leave to rise, about 1 hour. Meanwhile, preheat a grill (broiler) or heat a large ribbed skillet. Brush the sweet potato slices with oil and grill, turning once, brushing with oil as they cook, until coloured and tender. Repeat with the eggplant, zucchini and onion wedges.

PREHEAT the oven to 230°C (450°F). Punch down the dough, divide into two and roll each into 23 cm (9 in) rounds on a floured surface. Transfer to baking sheets. Brush the dough with oil and top with the grilled vegetables, then sprinkle with the sliced cheese, pine nuts and oregano. Cover loosely with plastic wrap and leave to rise in a warm place. Drizzle with a little oil. Bake in the oven for 10–15 minutes, or until the base is golden and crisp.

SERVES 4

PIZZA BASE

Sift the flour into a large bowl with the salt; stir in the sugar and yeast. Make a well in the centre and add the milk, egg and butter. Mix to a dough then turn out onto a well-floured board. Knead lightly for 4–5 minutes until smooth and elastic. Put the dough into a buttered bowl, turn it to coat with the butter and let it rise until doubled in bulk in a warm place, about 1 hour.

COMMERCIAL PIZZA BASE Acceptable pizza bases can be found in frozen food cabinets, however, once you practise yeast cookery a few times you will realise it is very easy—just allow an hour for the bread to rise—it is well worth it.

RIGHT: Roasted Vegetable and Goat's Cheese Pizza on a home-made base makes a more than agreeable lunch

LEEK AND TOMATO TARTE TATIN

A savoury relative of the well-loved French tarte Tatin, made with apples.
Zucchini (courgettes) or asparagus are also good prepared this way.

INGREDIENTS

2 tablespoons olive oil

15 g (½ oz) butter

1 sheet ready-rolled puff pastry

2 leeks, split in half lengthwise,
washed and green tops discarded

6 Roma (plum) tomatoes, halved

PREHEAT the oven to 200°C (400°F). Melt the butter and oil in a pan. You will need a cast-iron frying pan or a deep round shallow baking dish or saucepan that is flameproof and ovenproof. Arrange the leeks and tomatoes in the pan and place over a gentle heat and cook for about 5 minutes.

LAY out the pastry and cut into a circle a little larger than the top of the cooking pan. Place over leeks and tomatoes, allowing its edges to fall against the inside edge of the dish. Bake in the oven for 45 minutes to 1 hour. The tart is done when the pastry is crisp and golden. Invert the tart onto a warm serving plate.

SERVES 6–8

ASPARAGUS FRITTATA

The savoury omelette cakes of France, Italy and Spain make the perfect lunch
or picnic dish. Asparagus makes a superb frittata, but other vegetables can be used—
sliced zucchini, French beans, spinach leaves or sautéed mushrooms.

INGREDIENTS

1–2 bunches fresh asparagus, tough
ends removed and washed

2 tablespoons olive oil, plus a little
extra

1 clove garlic, crushed with salt

3 tablespoons water

6 large eggs

½ cup (60 g/2 oz) freshly grated
Parmesan cheese

freshly ground black pepper

a little freshly chopped oregano or
marjoram

HEAT a large frying pan and gently pan-fry the asparagus with the crushed garlic in the oil for about 5 minutes, uncovered, until softened and lightly coloured. Add the water and cook, half-covered, until asparagus is just tender, but still a little crisp. Remove from the pan and set aside.

MEANWHILE, lightly beat the eggs in a bowl and add the Parmesan, pepper and oregano or marjoram. Add a little more oil to the pan in which the asparagus was cooked and reheat. Pour in the egg mixture and cook over a moderate heat for 2 minutes. Arrange the asparagus spears decoratively on the eggs. Continue cooking until partially set, then place underneath a hot griller (broiler) until an even, light golden brown. Slice into wedges to serve, hot or cold.

SERVES 6–8

CLUB CHICKEN SALAD

The club sandwich is an American favourite, triple-decked with layers of chicken, bacon and tomatoes. Here's a salad version, the bread turns into crunchy croûtons to add a great texture contrast.

INGREDIENTS

3 cups cubed Italian bread

3 tablespoons olive oil

salt and freshly ground black pepper

6 rashers (slices) bacon, roughly chopped

750 g (1½ lb) chicken breasts, poached, skin and bones removed, and cut into bite-size pieces

1 punnet cherry tomatoes, halved

4 spring onions (scallions), including the green part, chopped

½ cup (125 mL/4 fl oz) basil mayonnaise (page 25)

large lettuce leaves, to serve

fresh basil sprigs, for garnish

PREHEAT the oven to 180°C (350°F). In a bowl, drizzle the bread cubes with the oil, tossing to coat evenly, and season with salt. Spread the bread cubes on a baking sheet, toast in the middle of the oven for about 15 minutes, or until golden, then cool. In a frying pan, cook the bacon over a moderate heat, tossing, until crisp. Transfer to absorbent paper towels to drain.

IN A large bowl, combine the chicken, half the tomatoes, the shallots, two-thirds of the bacon and the mayonnaise. Season with salt and pepper. Arrange the lettuce leaves on serving plates or bowls, and pile the chicken salad into each. Scatter with the croûtons and garnish each serving with the remaining bacon and tomatoes, and a basil sprig.

SERVES 6

WITLOF GRATIN

Lovely as a pre-theatre snack or light luncheon. I have been relaxed about the quantity of witlof. For some, one is just right, while others expect two per serve, they love them so much.

INGREDIENTS

6–8 heads witlof (Belgian endive)

6–8 thin slices raw or smoked ham

6–8 tablespoons grated Gruyère cheese

½ cup (125 mL/4 fl oz) fresh (light, single) cream

freshly grated nutmeg

PREHEAT the oven to 180°C (350°F). Drop the witlof into boiling, salted water for about 3 minutes. Drain, squeeze out excess water. Wrap each witlof in a ham slice and place in a buttered ovenproof dish. Sprinkle over the Gruyère, pour over the cream and season with a little grated nutmeg. Cook in the oven for 30 minutes.

SERVES 6

TOMATO HERB TART

Suitable for a light summer lunch, this tomato tart is made with a cheese pastry.
An even simpler version uses ready rolled puff pastry as a light and crispy base.

INGREDIENTS

1½ cups (185 g/6 oz) plain
(all-purpose) flour

pinch of salt

½ cup (60 g/2 oz) finely grated
cheddar cheese

1 tablespoon grated Parmesan
cheese

1 egg, beaten

60 g (2 oz) butter, softened

FILLING

375 g (12 oz) tomatoes, peeled and
sliced

2 tablespoons chopped fresh parsley

2 tablespoons chopped fresh basil
or thyme

freshly ground black pepper

1 tablespoon virgin olive oil

SIFT the flour and salt onto a board. Make a well in the centre, add the cheeses, egg and butter. Using the fingers of one hand, work the centre ingredients together and gradually work in the flour from the edge. Knead until smooth, form into a ball, cover with plastic wrap and chill for 1 hour.

MEANWHILE, preheat the oven to 200°C (400°F). Roll out the pastry and use to line a 23 cm (9 in.) square or round tart pan with a removable base. Trim the pastry edges, prick the base and chill for 20 minutes. Line with greaseproof paper and dried beans, and bake blind in the oven for 15 minutes. Remove the paper and beans, and return to the oven for 5 minutes.

LAYER the tomato slices in the pastry case, sprinkle each layer with herbs and pepper, and drizzle at the end with the virgin olive oil. Return to the oven for 5 minutes, until the tomatoes are hot and glistening. Leave to cool a few minutes before removing from pan to cool completely. The tart is best served at room temperature.

SERVES 6–8

READY ROLLED PUFF PASTRY

If using rolled-out commercial puff pastry, place on a dampened baking sheet and prick well with a fork. Leaving a 15 mm (½ in) edge free, sprinkle the surface with the grated cheddar and Parmesan cheese, and arrange the tomato slices and herbs over the top. Drizzle with the olive oil, season with pepper and bake in a preheated oven at 200°C (400°F) until pastry is puffed and golden, about 20 minutes. Serve hot or at room temperature.

LEFT: Tomato Herb Tart—warm and
fragrant—for a summer lunch when
vine-ripened tomatoes reach
perfection

WHAT'S FOR DINNER?

'WHAT'S for dinner?' poses no problems for the interested cook—whatever the decision, the food that is taken into those dedicated hands will be treated with reverence. What a joy for family and friends. Today's youth get quite sentimental about a roast dinner. I am often asked about how it's done, what are the secrets. It is this continuity with the past, some call it tradition, that lays hold on the imagination at the mention of a roast dinner. Within the past few years, however, something new has been happening to roast dinners. We are cooking lamb pink in the French manner or adopting a long, slow Moroccan way with tender lamb. We cook it on a bed of Mediterranean vegetables or as roasted in the Atlas Mountains by the Bedouins.

THE incomparable casseroles of England, ragoûts of France and braised meats of Europe made of beef, veal, lamb and poultry cooked in those wonderfully heavy pots, Dutch ovens and cocottes are as much loved today as a century ago. And for much the same reason.

THE focal point of many dinners is the noble meat, poultry or fish. Just as our imaginations and desires are stirred by the names of many dishes on restaurant menus, when enthusiastic cooks read recipes they can visualise the tastes, flavours and nuance of the finished dish.

ANYONE with a serious interest in food will appreciate a whole fish cooked over vine cuttings or fennel stalks, fish fillets deftly grilled or pan-fried in a crisp crust, fish soups with an Asian tang. Every food lover has discovered the joys of choice fish served carpaccio—paper-thin slices with a delectable dressing—or tartare with a sumptuous sauce.

ENTHUSIASTIC cooks will rise to the occasion of 'What's for dinner?' and produce a wonderful meal that all will acclaim as a salute to gastronomy and good living.

CHAPTER 5

ROAST DINNERS

Everyone loves a roast dinner, just like mother used to make. Here's how, but with an update, using the tenderest baby lamb, the most flavoursome beef and wonderful free-range chickens with all the accompaniments, sauces and gravies.

MOROCCAN ROAST LEG OF LAMB

If you like lamb pink, roast for 1¼–1½ hours; Moroccans like it well done, 2–2½ hours.

INGREDIENTS

*2 kg (4 lb) leg of lamb, wiped and
    trimmed*

*2–3 cloves garlic, peeled and cut
    into slivers*

2 teaspoons ground cumin

salt and freshly ground black pepper

3 tablespoons olive oil

*1 kg (2 lb) baby new potatoes or
    large potatoes, sliced thickly*

6 garlic cloves, whole and unpeeled

*2 medium eggplants (aubergines),
    cut into chunky pieces or 8 long
    finger ones, halved lengthwise*

*3 red or yellow capsicum (sweet
    peppers), cut into 4 pieces
    lengthwise and seeds discarded*

4–6 tomatoes, washed and halved

1 tablespoon chopped fresh oregano

PREHEAT the oven to 220°C (425°F). Pierce the lamb all over with the point of a sharp knife and insert the garlic slivers. Rub generously with the cumin, salt and pepper. Place the lamb on a wire rack fat side up in a large baking dish (roasting pan). Drizzle over the olive oil, add the potatoes and scatter over the whole garlic cloves and half the oregano. Put the lamb in the oven and reduce the heat to 180°C (350°F). Roast for 45 minutes. Add the eggplant to the baking dish of lamb with the capsicums and tomatoes. Turn the vegetables over in the olive oil, sprinkle with the remaining oregano and roast for a further 45 minutes. Baste the lamb and vegetables with the juices in the pan several times during cooking.

TO SERVE, cut the lamb into serving portions; pink lamb is best cut in thinner slices, across the grain. Arrange on a very hot platter with the vegetables. Offer little bowls of coarse salt and ground cumin for guests to season their lamb the Moroccan way.

SERVES 6–8

RIGANI

*Rigani, the wild marjoram of Greece, is sold dried throughout the world.
If unavailable, use fresh oregano or marjoram, or perhaps fresh thyme.*

ROAST LEG OF LAMB WITH PERSILLADE

One of the treats of spring is when young lambs come onto the market.
This leg is cooked in two stages in a hot oven, finished with a herby golden
crust. This is a French look at roast lamb, served a perfect, tender,
rosy medium rare.

INGREDIENTS

2 kg (4lb) leg of young lamb

salt and freshly ground black pepper

1–2 tablespoons olive oil

2–3 cloves garlic, peeled and finely
chopped

1 bunch of fresh parsley, flat-leaf
(Italian) or curly, finely chopped

2–3 sprigs fresh thyme

1½ cups (90 g/3 oz) fresh white
breadcrumbs

1 tablespoon softened butter

1 tablespoon Dijon mustard

PREHEAT the oven to 240°C (475°F). Rub a little salt and plenty of pepper into the leg of lamb. Put into a baking dish (roasting pan), brush with oil and roast in the oven for 50 minutes, or until the meat is rare—the centre of the joint will be rare, but not cold, when taken from the oven. Allow the meat to rest.

MEANWHILE, make the parsley coating. Mix together about ½ cup parsley, garlic, thyme, salt and pepper to taste, butter and breadcrumbs. Toss lightly. To finish the lamb, spread the cooled leg of lamb with the mustard. Cover with a thick, compact layer of breadcrumb mixture, pressing it on by hand. Return the lamb to the baking dish and roast for a further 15 minutes.

REMOVE the lamb from the oven and let it stand for 20 minutes before carving. The lamb should be a perfect rosy medium rare. Carve across the grain from the shank end, running the carving knife along the bone to lift off the cut slices.

LAMB done this way is good with Potatoes Dauphinoise Gratin (page 52) or crispy roast potatoes. Served on a bed of greens or watercress, the greens wilt but taste good with the delicious juices. This is, of course, a matter of taste.

SERVES 6–8

GARLIC-STUDDED LAMB Many people enjoy a garlic flavour running through a leg of lamb. Peel 3 cloves garlic and quarter lengthwise. With a small, sharp pointed knife, cut small but deep incisions in the meat and push in the garlic quarters. Garlic can still be added to the breadcrumb crust, depending on just how much garlic you wish to use.

RIGHT: Roast Leg of Lamb with Persillade has a herby, crisped golden crust which is crunchy and delicious

ROAST LEG OF LAMB

A baked dinner is very old-fashioned, but very good. For many of us, it is one of our fondest memories and keeps us going back to mother for more. There's a lot to do to get it on the table together with the vegetables and trimmings. If you've never orchestrated a complete roast dinner, now's the time.

INGREDIENTS

2 kg (4 lb) leg of lamb

salt and freshly ground black pepper

1 large clove garlic, peeled and sliced

6 small or 3 large potatoes

750 g (1½ lb) pumpkin (golden squash)

6 medium onions, peeled

sprigs of watercress or parsley, to garnish

GRAVY

2 teaspoons plain (all-purpose) flour

1½ cups (375 mL/12 fl oz) stock or vegetable water

RESTING MEATS

'Reposer' or 'resting' is a term you will find in many reference books. Roasted meats are 'rested' in a warm place for about 20 minutes before carving. This allows the juices to be reabsorbed by the tissues, giving the meat a succulent tenderness. Less juice escapes when it is carved and the slices tend to shrink less.

PREHEAT the oven to 200°C (400°F). Rub a little salt and pepper into the lamb. Cut 6–8 small incisions in the leg of lamb with a pointed knife. Push the garlic into the cuts in the lamb. Place the lamb on a wire rack in a baking dish (roasting pan). If the lamb is very lean, brush with 1–2 tablespoons olive oil. Roast in the oven for 20 minutes to sear the meat.

MEANWHILE, prepare the vegetables. Peel the potatoes and pumpkin, and cut the pumpkin into 6 portions about the same size as the potatoes. If using large potatoes, halve or quarter them, drop potatoes into boiling, salted water, cook for 7 minutes, then drain. Score the surface of the potatoes with a fork.

AT THE END of 20 minutes, remove the baking dish from the oven and baste the lamb well with the drippings in the pan. Place the parboiled potatoes, the pumpkin and onions around the meat in the dish and sprinkle with a little salt. Reduce oven heat to 180°C (350°F), return baking dish to the oven and cook for further 1–1¼ hours, basting the lamb every 20–30 minutes and turning the vegetables occasionally. To test, pierce the vegetables with a skewer. If still firm, leave a little longer and test again.

WHEN the lamb is cooked, remove from the oven and place on heated dish. Cover loosely with foil and keep warm, to rest the lamb before carving. Transfer the vegetables to another baking dish and roast in the oven at 200°C (400°F), for a further 10 minutes. Remove to a vegetable dish to serve. Meanwhile, make the gravy.

TO MAKE THE GRAVY, drain off all but 1 tablespoon fat from the pan. Place over a medium heat, stir in the flour and keep stirring until well browned. Add stock or vegetable water, and stir until mixture boils. Lower heat and simmer gently, stirring occasionally until it thickens. Strain into a gravy boat.

SERVES 6

TO CARVE THE LAMB, cut the meat into slices that are as thin or thick as desired, not parallel to the bone, but across the grain of the

TIMING FOR A ROAST OF LAMB

Allow a total roasting time of approximately 20 minutes per 500 g (1 lb), plus 20 minutes for lamb pink in the centre or 30 minutes for well-done lamb. A saddle of lamb or shoulder requires less time to cook. Always rest the lamb for 15–20 minutes in a turned-off oven with door ajar, or other warm place, before carving.

meat; as you work up from the shank end, the slices get larger. Cut several slices at a time along the bone to release the juices. Serve with gravy, roasted vegetables and sweet young green peas, with Mint Sauce on the side.

MINT SAUCE Combine 1 teaspoon sugar and 2 tablespoons chopped fresh mint. Add ½ cup (125 mL/4 fl oz) boiling water and 2 tablespoons malt vinegar, and allow to stand for 30 minutes or until required.

FRENCH ROASTING LAMB Prepare as above, but omit vegetables and cook as follows. Preheat the oven to 180°C (350°F). Place the lamb on a rack in a baking dish (roasting pan). Add ½ cup (125 mL/4 fl oz) white wine and ½ cup (125 mL/4 fl oz) water, 1 tablespoon butter and 1 teaspoon salt to the dish. Roast in the oven for 17–20 minutes per 500 g (1 lb). French lamb is always served underdone, with the flesh still pink. Baste lamb every 15 minutes.

ROAST POTATOES

Choose potatoes of medium and even sizes, or otherwise halve or quarter large ones. Use slightly yellow or white-fleshed potatoes, such as bison, coliban, patrone, sebago, russe, exton, kennebec or desirée. The fat may be vegetable or olive oil. Duck fat gives the potatoes a marvellous taste.

INGREDIENTS
6 medium potatoes, peeled
salt
oil, for roasting

PREHEAT the oven to 200°C (400°F). Place the potatoes in a medium-sized saucepan, cover with cold water and bring to the boil. Boil for 10 minutes. Drain and dry well in the saucepan. Run the tines of a fork over the surface of the potatoes and sprinkle lightly with salt. Put enough oil into a baking dish (roasting pan) to just cover the bottom. Heat the oil, then put in the potatoes and roast in the oven for 40–50 minutes, or until golden and crusty, turning and basting occasionally. Drain on absorbent paper towels.

IF YOU would like to roast the potatoes at the same time as the joint of meat, prepare as above, then place in the roasting pan alongside the joint during the last 45–60 minutes of cooking time, turning and basting with the pan juices.

ROAST STANDING RIB OF BEEF

A joint of beef should not be overseasoned, it has enough flavour in itself along with its traditional accompaniments. Gravy and a hot horseradish relish or hot English mustard are popular adjuncts. Serve roasted potatoes which can be baked in the hot oven as the beef stands 'resting'. This is one of the best meals in the world.

INGREDIENTS

1 standing rib of beef: 3 ribs will serve 6–8; 4 ribs will serve 8–10 or 1 rump of beef: 3 kg (6 lb) will serve 8; 2 kg (4 lb) will serve 6

1 teaspoon cracked black pepper

2 tablespoons olive oil

2 teaspoons sea salt

HOT ENGLISH MUSTARD

Mix 2 tablespoons hot dry English mustard powder with enough water to make a slack paste. Put into a small mustard pot.

HORSERADISH

Grate a fresh horseradish and mix with a little vinegar, or use a commercial grated horseradish. Some people like to mix it with a little cream to taste.

RIGHT: Roast Standing Rib of Beef with its traditional accompaniment, Yorkshire puddings

PREHEAT the oven to 220°C (425°F). Bring the beef to room temperature and rub the pepper over the surface. Heat a heavy flameproof baking dish (roasting pan) over a moderately high heat; when hot, add the oil and brown the beef on all sides. Place the beef, curved side up, in the dish; a rump should be placed on a wire rack in the baking dish. Press the salt onto the surface fat. Roast in the oven for 20 minutes, then reduce heat to 180°C (350°F) until done. For rare beef, allow 10–12 minutes per 500 g (1 lb); for medium rare, allow 15 minutes per 500 g (1 lb), plus 15 minutes; for well-done beef, allow 20 minutes per 500 g (1 lb), plus 20 minutes. Remove the beef from the baking dish to a warm plate, cover loosely with a double sheet of foil and leave to rest for 20–30 minutes in a warm place.

TO MAKE GRAVY, pour off all but 2 tablespoons fat from the baking dish. Over a moderate heat, deglaze the pan with ½ cup (125 mL/4 fl oz) white wine and 1 tablespoon sherry vinegar, lifting off the brown bits. Add 2 cups (500 mL/16 fl oz) beef stock and any red juices from the meat; cook for a few minutes. Season to taste with salt and freshly ground black pepper. Strain into a small saucepan and, just before serving, swirl in 2 teaspoons butter—this softens the gravy and creates a liaison. Pour into a gravy boat to serve.

YORKSHIRE PUDDINGS Sift 1 cup (125 g/4 oz) plain (all-purpose) flour and 1 teaspoon salt into a bowl. Make a well in the centre, add 1 large or 2 small beaten eggs and 1¼ cups (310 mL/ 10 fl oz) milk, beating the centre well and gradually incorporating all the flour. Pour into a jug and refrigerate until required. When you take the roast out of the oven, increase the heat to 200°C (400°F). Heat 8–12 Yorkshire pudding or muffin pans. Put a good teaspoon of the hot meat drippings into each pan, give the batter a good beat and pour into the pans, filling them about two-thirds full. Bake in the oven for 20 minutes, reduce heat to 180°C (375°F) and cook a further 5–10 minutes.

ROAST CHICKEN

*Roast chicken dinner, home cooked, is worth travelling miles for,
especially on a Sunday. It is also worth buying a large free-range roasting chicken.
Don't miss the gravy—cream or mushroom are both recommended or, for a
touch of nostalgia, the lovely English Bread Sauce (right). What goes
well with a roast chicken dinner? Start with Tomato
Saffron Soup (page 20).*

INGREDIENTS

1.8 kg (3½ lb) free-range chicken

*45g (½ oz) butter or 2 tablespoons
olive oil*

salt and freshly ground black pepper

*small bunch fresh tarragon or
parsley*

3 strips orange peel (rind)

*1 cup (250 mL/8 fl oz) chicken
stock (page 12)*

*500 g (1 lb) baby new potatoes or
4 large potatoes, peeled and
quartered*

½ cup (125 mL/4 fl oz) white wine

*1 tablespoon plain (all-purpose)
flour*

TRUSSING A CHICKEN

*To truss, put chicken on its back
and cut a small hole for the tail to
push through to close vent. Pull
skin over neck and secure by
folding wing tips back over skin.
Run string around wings, cross over
the back, turn chicken and tie legs
together, keeping them close to
the body.*

PREHEAT the oven to 200°C (400°F). Remove all the loose fat from the chicken and wipe inside and out with paper towels. Put half the butter or oil, salt and pepper to taste, tarragon or parsley, and strips of orange rind inside the chicken. Truss in a neat shape (see hint). Rub the chicken all over with the remaining butter or oil and put the chicken on its side on a roasting rack, if you have one, in a baking dish (roasting pan) with ½ cup (125 mL/4 fl oz) stock and the potatoes. Roast in the oven for 20 minutes, turn on the other side and baste well with stock. Turn potatoes.

REDUCE the heat to 190°C (375°F) and continue to roast, turning and basting every 20 minutes and adding more stock as necessary. Towards the end of cooking, add the wine. Turn the potatoes from time to time. There should be just enough stock to keep the juice in the pan from scorching.

COOK for 1–1¼ hours or until the chicken is done, turning the bird on its back for the last 15 minutes to brown the breast. To test, run a fine skewer into the thigh joint of chicken. If the juice that runs out is pink, the chicken is not quite cooked, but if it is clear and colourless, it is ready. Remove the chicken from the pan and remove string. Allow the chicken to stand in a warm place for 15 minutes before carving. Remove the vegetables and keep warm while making the gravy.

CUT the chicken into joints in the kitchen. Arrange on a heated serving dish, surrounded with potatoes. Serve with minted fresh peas, baby carrots or other young cooked green vegetables, and any of the following gravies.

TO MAKE GRAVY Pour off all but 2 tablespoons juices from the pan. Add the flour and stir well until lightly browned. Add the remaining chicken stock or stock and water to make 1½ cups (375 mL/12 fl oz); stir until thickened. Season with salt and pepper. Keep warm in a small saucepan or a gravy boat.

SERVES 6

CREAM GRAVY Make as for gravy, but just before serving stir in 3 tablespoons fresh (single, light) cream and cook a little until thickened.

MUSHROOM CREAM GRAVY Pour off all but 2 tablespoons juices from the pan. Add 8–10 sliced button mushrooms to the pan. Cook gently for about 3–4 minutes, stirring and turning together to cook evenly. Proceed as for gravy, stirring in 3 tablespoons fresh (single, light) cream at the end.

MEDITERRANEAN CHICKEN

Here's a way of adding the sunny robust flavours of the Mediterranean to roast chicken. Prepare the chicken as for Roast Chicken, but use olive oil in place of the butter.

GARNISH

½ cup (75 g/2½ oz) green or *black olives*

12–16 button mushrooms

6 long finger eggplants (aubergines), trimmed and halved

4–6 ripe tomatoes

6–8 cloves garlic, peeled

fresh parsley or *watercress, to garnish*

PREPARE as for Roast Chicken. While cooking the chicken, prepare the garnish. Pit olives, if liked, either with a cherry stoner or by cutting flesh from the pit in very much the same way as you would peel an orange. Use a small pointed knife and only keep the point of the knife on the pit. Wipe the mushrooms carefully with a damp cloth. Place the olives, mushrooms, eggplant, tomatoes and garlic around the chicken for the last 20 minutes of cooking, pushing the potatoes to one side. Serve the chicken surrounded by vegetables. Garnish with parsley or watercress.

SERVES 6

ROAST CHICKEN NICOISE Roast the bird as for Mediterranean chicken, but add 2–3 tablespoons olive oil, 3–4 zucchini (courgettes) cut into chunks, 2 onions peeled and quartered and 1 red or green capsicum (sweet pepper), quartered and seeded. This is a kind of ratatouille mixture of vegetables giving it its French name, *ratatouille*, which means tossed or tumbled together.

ROAST LEG OR LOIN OF PORK

It was a great celebration the day I learned to cook roast pork with crispy crackling and tender, succulent meat the way mother used to do it.

INGREDIENTS

1 loin of pork, weighing 2 kg (4 lb) boned or left on the bone with the chops chined or 1 leg of pork, boned and tied, or piece from leg

coarse sea salt or cooking salt

2 cloves garlic, peeled and slivered

4 potatoes (russet Burbank, pontiac, sebagos are all good for roasting)

2 sweet potatoes

APPLE SAUCE

Peel, core and quarter 2 Granny Smith apples. Simmer with ½ cup (125 mL/4 fl oz) water, 2 whole cloves and 1 teaspoon sugar in a covered saucepan until the apples are tender and fluffy. Mash with a fork, add ½ teaspoon grated lemon rind.

LEFT: Roast Loin of Pork with crunchy crackling—some say the best part

ASK the butcher to score the skin of the pork at 5 mm (¼ in.) intervals or in a diamond pattern. Preheat the oven to 230°C (450°F). Rub the pork all over with salt. Pierce through the fat with a sharp pointed knife and insert a sliver of garlic; repeat over surface at regular intervals to use up all the garlic. Place the pork, skin side up, on a rack in a baking dish (roasting pan). Roast for 30 minutes or until the skin is looking crispy and golden. Reduce the heat to 180°C (350°F) and roast until cooked through, allowing 25 minutes per 500 g (1 lb), about 2 hours in all. Allow an extra 30 minutes if roasting a leg or for a well-done loin.

WHILE the pork is roasting, peel the potatoes—halve if medium sized or quarter if large. Peel the sweet potatoes and cut into pieces. Parboil for 7 minutes in boiling, salted water, drain and score the surface with a fork. Scatter around the pork for the last 25 minutes of cooking, turning every now and then.

REMOVE the baking dish from oven. Transfer the pork to a large plate for 20 minutes. Keep warm—this resting period helps the meat and juices 'set' for easy carving. Transfer the potatoes, sweet potatoes and some of the fat to a small baking dish, return to the oven and crisp the potatoes while you make the gravy and cook some green vegetables. The apple sauce can be made ahead.

TO SERVE, remove the crackling. Slice the meat across the grain—in cutlets if the loin was roasted or slices of leg. Each serving gets pork meat, some crackling, a few roasted potatoes and sweet potatoes, gravy and some apple sauce to cut the rich, fatty meat.

SERVES 8

GRAVY Pour off all but 1 tablespoon fat, place the baking dish over a medium heat, sprinkle in 2 teaspoons plain (all-purpose) flour and keep stirring until well browned. Add 1½ cups (375 mL/12 fl oz) vegetable stock or half white wine and water. Stir until mixture boils, reduce the heat and simmer gently, stirring the gravy occasionally until it thickens. Strain.

FRENCH ROASTED CHICKEN WITH GREEN PEPPERCORNS

Use a free-range chicken for this superb dish if you can. Pungent green peppercorns and butter are slipped under the skin and release their aromatic flavour into the bird as it roasts.

INGREDIENTS

1 roasting chicken, about 1.5 kg (3 lb)

1 lemon, halved

60 g (2 oz) butter

2 teaspoons green peppercorns

1½ cups (375 mL/12 fl oz) white wine or *chicken stock*

salt

PREHEAT the oven to 220°C (425°F). Remove the neck and excess fat from the chicken. Wipe inside and out with absorbent paper towels, then rub over the surface with the cut lemon. Mix half the butter with the green peppercorns and push through the neck end gently, between the skin and the breasts and down into the thighs, working it over evenly. Tie the legs together. Rub the remaining butter over the skin of the chicken and place the chicken in a baking dish (roasting pan), on a roasting rack if you have one. Pour in 1 cup (250 mL/8 fl oz) wine or stock. Sprinkle the chicken lightly with salt. Cover with a piece of buttered paper and roast in the oven for 15 minutes. Reduce the heat to 190°C (375°F) and continue cooking, basting occasionally with the juices and turning the chicken from time to time. Add a little water if the juices seem to be drying out. The chicken should be turned on its back for the final 15 minutes to brown the breast. When cooked, remove the chicken to a warm dish and stand in a warm place while you make the sauce.

SKIM any fat from the pan juices then add the remaining wine or stock. Simmer over a high heat, scraping any brown bits from the bottom of the pan, until the sauce has reduced a little. Strain into a gravy boat. Place the chicken, whole or cut into serving pieces, on a heated platter. Pour a little sauce over the chicken. Reserve some sauce to hand around. Serve with roast potatoes (page 73) or crusty bread and a green salad.

SERVES 4–6

TARRAGON CHICKEN Prepare as for French Roasted Chicken above, but use 2 teaspoons dried tarragon in place of the green peppercorns. If fresh tarragon is available put a few sprigs in the cavity and add 6–8 torn leaves in the sauce. Still use the dried leaves in the breast for a full flavour.

CHAPTER 6

ONE-POT COOKING

One-pot cooking is not new. Generations of cooks have used
those wonderful casseroles, cocottes, daubières and Dutch ovens to
create culinary masterpieces. These pots may be earthenware, cast-iron
with enamel coating, copper with a stainless steel or tin lining. Most are
flameproof, some pottery and stoneware, glazed on the inside and some on
the outside, too; these are recommended for use in the oven. What links
these wonderful pieces of equipment is that the food simmers gently
in its own flavoursome juices, developing the rich flavours and
heady smell that is so enticing when the lid is taken off.
Such a comfort for today's busy cook.

CHICKEN FORRESTIERE

*Wild mushrooms from the forest give this dish of braised chicken pieces its name.
Wild mushrooms are now cultivated and there are many from which to choose.*

INGREDIENTS

1.8 kg (3½ lb) chicken

3 tablespoons plain (all-purpose)
  flour

¼ teaspoon paprika

salt and freshly ground pepper

60 g (2 oz) butter

8–10 button mushrooms or *wood*
  mushrooms such as Swiss browns,
  slippery jacks

8 baby carrots, scraped

12 small onions, peeled

8 baby new potatoes

1 bouquet garni

1½ cups (375 mL/12 fl oz) chicken
  stock

½ cup (125 mL/4 fl oz) white wine

3 tablespoons fresh (single, light)
  cream

PREHEAT the oven to 180°C (350°F). Joint the chicken into thighs,
drumsticks, wings with a bit of breast and breast, keeping in the bone.
Mix the flour with the paprika and a little salt and pepper. Coat the
chicken pieces in the flour mixture. Melt the butter in a large frying
pan and brown the chicken pieces on all sides, then transfer to a
casserole or Dutch oven.

WIPE the mushrooms with a damp cloth. Add the carrots, onions
and mushrooms to the pan and cook until golden. Add the vegetables
to the chicken with the potatoes and bouquet garni. Pour some stock
into the pan and scrape up any brown bits; pour this and the
remaining stock and wine over the chicken. Cover and cook in the
oven for about 1¼ hours, or until the chicken and vegetables are
tender. Discard the bouquet garni. Stir in the cream just before
serving.

SERVES 4

CHICKEN WITH ARTICHOKES

*This dish has all the flavour of long, slow cooking yet takes only 45 minutes—
that's a plus for today's tender chickens. Use artichokes marinated in olive oil
for this dish, any good delicatessen stocks them; best of all, use fresh globe artichokes
when in season. I also use a free-range chicken; so good and flavoursome.*

INGREDIENTS

1 tablespoon olive oil

30 g (1 oz) butter

*1 roasting chicken, about 1.5 kg
  (3 lb) or slightly larger, jointed*

salt and freshly ground black pepper

*4 young fresh globe artichokes,
  prepared, or 6–8 artichokes,
  marinated in oil*

6 tablespoons white wine

pinch of saffron threads

12 black olives

*⅓ cup (90 mL/3 fl oz) fresh (single,
  light) cream*

HEAT the oil and butter in a large sauté pan, deep-sided frying pan or Dutch oven. Arrange the chicken in the pan with the skin-side facing down. Season with salt and pepper, cover and cook gently for about 5 minutes, turning once or twice. Now add the fresh artichokes, wine, saffron and olives, and cook, covered, for a further 30 minutes. If using marinated artichokes, add them now and cook for a further 15 minutes.

REMOVE the chicken, artichokes and olives to a warm serving dish. Add the cream to the pan, heat for a minute or two swirling the pan around until the sauce is syrupy. Spoon the sauce over the chicken. Serve with boiled new potatoes which have been tossed in butter until lightly brown.

SERVES 4–6

TO JOINT A CHICKEN First remove the legs, then cut off the drumsticks using a sharp knife. Detach the wings then divide the carcass in two, removing the back, but not cutting through the breast. Cut through the breast bone then cut each half-breast in two. Keep the back and neck for stock. Trim the chicken pieces, removing any excess fat.

RIGHT: Chicken with Artichokes—fresh or marinated artichokes may be used in this superb dish

---

FRESH ARTICHOKES

Cut the top third of the artichoke clean off, then begin trimming off the coarse outer leaves. Leave 5 cm (2 in.) of stalk at the base, paring around the heart until you reach the tender inner leaves. As each artichoke is prepared, drop it into a large bowl of cold water acidulated with the juice of 1 lemon. Halve or quarter if large, drop into boiling, salted water and cook for 10 minutes if using in above recipe.

CHICKEN WITH GARLIC PUREE

When a recipe for chicken using 40 cloves of garlic first appeared I was intrigued but wary, only to discover that the garlic was surprisingly mild and delicious. This recipe is a variation, but very good, the 4 bulbs of garlic are cooked to a soft purée and served as a side sauce. Another way of serving the chicken is with a creamy purée of potatoes and garlic recipe (below).

INGREDIENTS

*1 roasting chicken, about 1.5 kg
  (3 lb) or slightly larger, preferably
  cornfed or free-range*
*2 sprigs fresh rosemary or
  ½ teaspoon dried oregano*
2 sprigs fresh parsley
salt and freshly ground black pepper
*2 tablespoons olive oil, plus
  4 teaspoons extra*
4 heads of young, fresh garlic
*2 tablespoons extra virgin olive oil
  or fresh (single, light) cream*
freshly chopped parsley

PREHEAT the oven to 180°C (350°F). Wipe the chicken and season, including the cavity, with rosemary or oregano, parsley, salt and pepper. Truss into a neat shape with string. Heat 2 tablespoons olive oil in a deep, flameproof casserole dish and add the chicken, turning until golden all over. Cut off excess stalks and excess papery skin from the garlic, put each of the garlic heads in a square of foil, add a teaspoon of olive oil to each and bring up the edges of the foil to make a loose, but well-sealed parcel. Place parcels around the chicken.

COVER the casserole and cook in the oven for 1¼ hours. Lift out the chicken to rest on a warmed serving dish in a warm place—the turned-off oven, with the door ajar, is a good place; the serving plates can be put in the oven to warm at the same time.

TAKE the foil garlic parcels from the casserole, open and squeeze each garlic clove between your thumb and index finger to extract the garlic (use a fine rubber kitchen glove if you don't want your fingers to get too smelly!). Mash the garlic to a purée, using any oil and juice from the packets. Add the extra virgin olive oil or cream, stir through and put into a small bowl to accompany the chicken. To serve, joint the chicken and serve on heated plates with crusty bread or purée of potatoes and the garlic sauce on the side. Sprinkle with fresh parsley.

SERVES 4

POTATO PUREE WITH GARLIC

For this splendid dish, cook the chicken and garlic as above. While cooking the dish, boil 750 g (1½ lb) peeled potatoes until tender, drain and mash well, adding ½ cup (125 mL/4 fl oz) hot milk. Add 1–2 tablespoons of the garlic purée and beat to a smooth purée. Serve with the chicken. The remaining garlic purée may be offered in a small dish for those who are garlic addicts. For another version of this delectable purée, see page 96.

CHICKEN CASSEROLE WITH GOLDEN DELICIOUS

Apples and apple cider are used in this classic dish. The golden delicious apple, with its crisp, sweet, aromatic flesh, is used to advantage in chicken dishes in France, the USA and Australia. Try them in this casserole; you can use apples of your choice, such as Granny Smiths.

INGREDIENTS

1 roasting chicken, preferably cornfed or free-range, or 6–8 chicken
joints

45 g (1½ oz) butter

8–10 baby onions or golden
shallots, peeled and left whole

2 rashers (slices) bacon, cut into
thick strips

2 golden delicious apples, peeled
and cored, and cut into eighths

1 cup (250 mL/8 fl oz) apple cider

salt and freshly ground black pepper

bouquet of fresh herbs such as
parsley, lemon thyme, bay leaf

2 extra golden delicious apples,
cored and cut into six wedges
(optional)

PREHEAT the oven to 160°C (325°). Cut the chicken into serving joints (see page 82). Heat the butter in a flameproof casserole and brown the chicken pieces, a few at a time, until browned on each side. Remove and set aside. Add the onions or shallots to the casserole and sauté over a gentle heat. Add the bacon, increase the heat and, when coloured, add the apple that has been cut into eighths. Shake over a brisk heat for a minute or two, then remove from the casserole. Add the cider to the pan, letting it bubble for a minute.

ARRANGE the chicken pieces in layers in the casserole, spooning over the apples, onions or shallots, and bacon, adding plenty of salt and pepper. Add the herbs and cover the casserole tightly. Cook in the oven for 1–1¼ hours. Serve the chicken from the casserole. If liked, you can pan-fry the extra apple wedges in butter for several minutes, just enough to heat through and release the fresh apple flavours. Serve with the casserole.

SERVES 4–6

NOTE Beurre bosc or nashi pears could also be used in this recipe. Of course, they add a different, but interesting taste.

VEAL RAGOUT PROVENCAL

INGREDIENTS

3 onions, chopped

3 large cloves garlic, crushed

¼ cup (60 mL/2 fl oz) olive oil

1 kg (2 lb) boneless veal shoulder,
    cut into 5 cm (2 in.) pieces

4 strips orange rind

4 large tomatoes, peeled, seeded and
    quartered

1 cup (250 mL/8 fl oz) white wine

2 sprigs fresh rosemary, plus extra
    for garnish

250 g (8 oz) golden shallots,
    blanched and skins slipped off

250 g (8 oz) carrots, cut into
    julienne

salt and freshly ground pepper

½ cup (75 g/2½ oz) black olives

IN A large flameproof casserole, cook the onions and two-thirds of the garlic in the oil over a moderately low heat, stirring until softened. Add the veal, 2 strips orange rind, tomatoes, wine and rosemary. Bring to the boil. Cover and braise the stew over a low heat for 1¼ hours, until tender. Stir in the golden shallots, carrot and julienne of orange rind cut from the remaining orange rind. Simmer for a further 15 minutes. Just before serving, add the remaining garlic; season with salt and pepper. Garnish with the olives and extra rosemary torn into small sprigs.

SERVES 6

NOTE The French have a great affection for their ragoûts—the equivalent of our braise or casserole. The long, slow cooking of a ragoût produces a velvety, tender meat. Orange rind is a common seasoning in Provençal food—it certainly sets off this superb veal ragoût.

DILL LAMB SHOULDER

INGREDIENTS

1 shoulder lamb, boned

salt and freshly ground pepper

10 sprigs fresh dill, stalks removed

2 teaspoons salt

12 cups (3 litres/4¾ imp. pints)
    water

1 tablespoon plain (all-purpose)
    flour

1 tablespoon lemon juice

RIGHT: Veal Ragout Provençal—wine, herbs and orange peel give this ragoût French flair

SEASON the cut surface of the lamb with salt and pepper. Place 4 sprigs dill in the lamb; roll up the lamb and tie to keep a good shape. Place the lamb in a large saucepan, add salt and pour the water over the top. Simmer for 10 minutes. Skim, then add 4 sprigs dill. Cover the pan and simmer for 1½ hours or until tender. Remove and keep warm. Skim off any fat and use some of the stock to make the dill sauce. Blend the flour with a little water and use to thicken 1½ cups (375 mL/12 fl oz) lamb stock. Add the lemon juice and remaining 2 sprigs dill, snipped. Carve the lamb and serve with the dill sauce. Accompany with steamed new potatoes and vegetables in season.

SERVES 6

BEEF RAGOUT WITH WOOD MUSHROOMS

*The French make the most marvellous casseroles, using inexpensive
cuts of meat to great advantage. Shin (shank) of beef is cut into large pieces
and simmered gently in paprika, pepper, mushrooms and
turnips until tender.*

INGREDIENTS

45 g (1½ oz) butter

1 medium onion, chopped

1 clove garlic

*1 kg (2 lb) shin (shank) of beef, cut
into large cubes, about 5 cm
(2 in.)*

2 teaspoons paprika

salt and freshly ground black pepper

2 tablespoons tomato paste

1 cup (250 mL/8 fl oz) water

*250 g (8 oz) fresh mushrooms,
button, Swiss browns or
slippery jacks*

*2 white turnips, peeled and diced,
or 12 baby turnips, trimmed*

*1 tablespoon each butter and plain
(all-purpose) flour, blended*

MUSHROOMS

*Mushrooms make a difference to the
flavour of many dishes. White
buttons are used for a delicate finish,
open flat field mushrooms give a
more rustic taste and wood
mushrooms such as Swiss browns or
slippery jacks lend their own rich
flavour and texture.*

HEAT the butter in a large, heavy flameproof casserole or pan. Add the onion and garlic, and sauté until the onion is transparent. Discard garlic. Add the meat, paprika, salt and pepper. Cook over a moderate heat, stirring, until meat is browned. This may be done in several batches. Return the meat to the casserole. Add the tomato paste and water. Cover and simmer very gently for 1 hour. Add the mushrooms and turnips, and continue to simmer gently until the meat is tender. The total cooking time is about 1½ hours. When meat is tender, add blended butter and flour, bit by bit, stirring constantly until liquid is thickened to your liking. Serve with steamed rice, buttered noodles or polenta. Follow with a peppery watercress salad.

SERVES 6

WATERCRESS SALAD This is the perfect finish to this rich ragoût. Pick over a large bunch of watercress, removing tough stalks. Put the sprigs in a bowl, wash well and shake dry. Put in a salad bowl and toss in 2 tablespoons virgin olive oil and 1 teaspoon balsamic vinegar, salt and freshly ground black pepper.

NOTE Shin (shank) of beef is often called gravy beef. It is an inexpensive cut, but the best for long, slow cooking. It has a good gelatinous quality that gives the finished dish the succulence that makes a ragoût so delicious.

LEEK AND LAMB RAGOUT

Lamb neck chops are sweet and succulent; they produce some of the best dishes ever to come out of the kitchen.

INGREDIENTS

750 g (1¼ lb) *middle* or *best neck lamb chops*

½ cup (60 g/2 oz) plain (all-purpose) flour, seasoned with salt and freshly ground black pepper

30 g (1 oz) butter

3 leeks, well washed and cut into 5 cm (2 in.) pieces

1 × 410 g (13 fl oz) can tomatoes or 4 tomatoes, peeled and seeded

1¼ cups (310 mL/10 fl oz) water or stock

2 teaspoons chopped mixed herbs such as parsley, thyme, oregano

freshly chopped parsley, to garnish

PREHEAT the oven to 160°C (325°F). Toss the lamb in the seasoned flour. Melt the butter in a large pan and brown the lamb on all sides. Place in a casserole. Sauté the leeks gently for 2 minutes in the same pan used for the lamb. Drain the canned tomatoes, reserving the juice; halve and flick out the seeds, then add to the casserole with the leeks. Add any remaining flour to the fat in the pan and cook for 1 minute. Stir in water or stock, reserved tomato juice and herbs. Season with salt and pepper. Bring to the boil, stirring. Pour over the lamb. Cover and cook in the oven for 2–2½ hours. Adjust seasoning before serving. Strew with some freshly chopped parsley and serve with steamed potatoes or crusty bread.

SERVES 4

M'CHOUI OF LAMB

One of the best lamb dishes I've ever had, from Berber country in the Atlas mountains.

INGREDIENTS

1 shoulder of lamb

30 g (1 oz) butter, softened

2 cloves garlic, chopped

1 teaspoon sea salt

1 teaspoon ground cumin

1 teaspoon ground paprika

¼ teaspoon cayenne pepper

1 tablespoon olive oil

½ cup (125 mL/4 fl oz) water

bunches of fresh mint, coriander (Chinese parsley) and watercress

TRIM any excess fat from the lamb and cut off the shank. Cut a few incisions on the upper and underside of the lamb. Blend the butter with the garlic, salt, cumin, paprika and cayenne into a paste; rub well into the meat, including the shank. Set aside for several hours. Heat the oil in a heavy flameproof casserole or Dutch oven. Place the lamb fat side down and brown. Turn over, add the water, cover and reduce the heat to low. Pot-roast for 2–2½ hours, or cook in the oven at 150°C (300°F). To serve, place the lamb on a hot platter. Garnish with the sprigs of fresh mint, coriander and watercress. Offer small bowls of sea salt and ground cumin, and eat with a flat bread such as pita or Turkish pide.

SERVES 3–4

SHOULDER OF LAMB WITH FENNEL

People who know claim the shoulder of lamb is one of the best cuts to roast or pot-roast. This is a good example of making the most of this prime cut. The lovely aniseed flavour of fennel adds interest; when Florence fennel (finocchio) is not in season, replace with a similiar quantity of onions, tender herbs or celery. It is a very good dish whichever vegetable you use.

INGREDIENTS

1 small shoulder of lamb, boned

3 cloves garlic, cut in slivers

125 g (4 oz) pork fat or fatty bacon, cut into short strips

½ teaspoon grated lemon rind

3–4 tarragon sprigs, chopped, or 1 teaspoon dried tarragon

salt and freshly ground black pepper

3 tablespoons olive oil

1 teaspoon sugar

½ cup (125 mL/4 fl oz) water

1 large or 2 small Florence fennel (finocchio) bulbs, trimmed and quartered

4–6 small scrubbed potatoes such as small pink-eye or kipfler

3 carrots, thickly sliced

2 teaspoons potato flour or plain (all-purpose) flour

a little water (extra)

ORDER a small shoulder of lamb boned but not rolled from your butcher. Lay the shoulder out on a work surface, cut side up. Strew the strips of pork fat or bacon over the cut side of the lamb along with the lemon rind and half the tarragon. Season with salt and pepper. Roll the lamb shoulder up and tie.

HEAT the oil in a heavy flameproof casserole or pan, brown the shoulder on all sides, sprinkle in the sugar to brown then add the water. Add the fennel, potatoes, carrots and remaining tarragon. Cover, lower the heat and cook gently, turning the food every now and then, for 1–1¼ hours.

REMOVE the meat and vegetables to a heated platter. Mix the flour with a little water and pour very slowly into the liquid in the pan, stirring hard with a wire whisk. Spoon the sauce over the meat or serve from the casserole. The meat is cut in generous slices; this can be done at the table or in the kitchen.

SERVES 6

LEFT: Shoulder of Lamb with Fennel can cook gently while you relax with family and friends

BRAISED LAMB SHANKS

We all know that the meat nearest the bone is the sweetest. When a visiting international chef to a top hotel had lamb shanks on his menu, everyone raved about this old-fashioned cut. They were superb. Think about them for your next dinner party.

INGREDIENTS

6 lamb shanks, nobbly ends
* cut off*
plain (all-purpose) flour, for
* dredging*
salt and freshly ground black pepper
1 tablespoon chopped fresh oregano
* or 1 teaspoon dried*
⅓ cup (90 mL/3 fl oz) light
* olive oil*
grated rind of 1 lemon
1 medium onion, chopped
1 cup diced white turnips
1 cup diced carrots
1 clove garlic
2 tomatoes, peeled, seeded and
* quartered*
¾ cup (185 mL/6 fl oz) red wine
¾ cup (185 mL/6 fl oz) stock—beef,
* veal or chicken (page 12)*
1 tablespoon plain (all-purpose)
* flour*
2 teaspoons butter, softened

ASK the butcher to cut the nobbly end knuckles off the shanks, but do not discard. Preheat the oven to 180°C (350°F). Wipe the lamb shanks with a damp cloth. Dredge with the flour, season with salt and pepper, and press oregano onto the surface.

HEAT the oil in a frying pan and brown the shanks a few at a time. Transfer to a large casserole and sprinkle with the lemon rind. Add the onion, turnip, carrot and garlic to the frying pan and cook, stirring, for 5 minutes. Add the tomatoes, wine and stock, and boil, stirring well, for a few minutes. Pour the contents of the pan over the meat in the casserole; top with the reserved knuckles which give a gelatinous quality.

COVER and bake in the oven for 1½ hours or until meat is tender. Remove the shanks and keep warm; discard the knuckles. Thicken gravy with the flour blended with the butter, adding this a little at a time until you have the consistency you want. Serve the shanks with some of the sauce and creamy mashed potatoes or boiled rice.

SERVES 6

LAMB SHANKS WITH BARLEY This is a wholesome, old-fashioned soupy broth just like my Scottish mother used to make. Make as above using a large pot and only 3 lamb shanks and 8 cups (2 litres/3¼ imp. pints) water in place of the wine and stock. Add 6 tablespoons rinsed pearl barley. Simmer gently for 1½ hours. Remove the shanks and cut meat into small pieces; return to the pot. Serve in shallow soup bowls topped with freshly chopped parsley.

SERVES 4–6

POTATO MOUSSAKA

Moussaka is made in many Mediterranean countries, each with a slight variation. The main ingredients however, remain the same—minced lamb or beef, potato or eggplant (aubergine), and a custard-like topping. It takes a little time to assemble, but is well worth the effort. Long, slow cooking is required for this dish to be really good.

INGREDIENTS

4 *medium potatoes*

4 *tablespoons olive oil*

375 g (¾ *lb*) *minced* (*ground*) *lamb or lean minced steak* (*ground beef*)

1 *large onion, finely chopped*

1 *clove garlic, finely chopped*

1 *tablespoon chopped fresh oregano or* 1 *teaspoon dried*

1 × 400 g (13 *oz*) *can peeled tomatoes, chopped*

½–1 *cup* (125–250 *mL/4–8 fl oz*) *water*

salt and freshly ground black pepper

1 *cup* (250 *mL/8 fl oz*) *milk*

3 *eggs, lightly beaten*

4 *tablespoons freshly grated Parmesan cheese*

PREHEAT the oven to 180°C (350°F). Put the potatoes in a large saucepan and cover with water. Bring to the boil and cook for 10–12 minutes or until tender. Drain and, when cool enough to handle, peel and cut the potatoes into slices.

MEANWHILE, heat the oil in heavy nonstick frying pan and sauté the meat and onion over a medium heat for 5 minutes, stirring to break up the meat. Add the garlic, oregano, tomatoes, couscous and water, and season with salt and pepper. Cover and simmer gently for 12 minutes, stirring from time to time.

IN A mixing bowl, whisk the milk and eggs together and season with salt and pepper. Line a buttered 8-cup (2 litre/3¼ imp. pint) casserole with half the potato slices. Spoon the meat mixture into the casserole, then cover this with a layer of the remaining potatoes. Pour the milk mixture evenly over the top and sprinkle over the Parmesan cheese.

BAKE in the oven for 45 minutes. Serve hot or cold, cut into generous squares or wedges, and accompanied by a green salad.

SERVES 4

MOUSSAKA WITH EGGPLANT Eggplant (aubergine) with its lovely purple skin mades a wonderful moussaka. Using the above recipe, replace potato slices with aubergine, 1 large or 2 medium. Cut the aubergine in thick slices, score slices lightly and place in a ceramic or glass dish. Sprinkle the slices liberally with salt. Cover with a plate and leave for an hour. Rinse slices and pat dry. Heat 4 tablespoons olive oil in a frying pan (skillet) and fry the aubergine slices on each side. You may have to add more oil. Proceed with the recipe, layering the eggplant slices as for potatoes.

CHAPTER 7

POULTRY AND GAME

Chicken can be roasted or baked, or jointed and grilled or pan-fried. It readily takes to spices, herbs, lemon, wine, mushrooms, rice and pasta. It is amazing what can be done with a chicken. Quail and ducklings, too, keep our interest alive in these delicious birds. One important word, a free-range, fresh bird is best. One that has scratched and pecked around, and had some sort of life—the best and most passionate cooks agree.

SPICED BUTTERY CHICKEN

A different and delicious way of pan-frying chicken. Aromatic spices are added in two stages, and finished with a buttery sauce.

INGREDIENTS

2 half chicken breasts

2 chicken marylands (thigh with leg attached)

juice of 2 lemons

1 teaspoon salt

2 teaspoons paprika

45 g (1½ oz) unsalted butter

¼ teaspoon saffron threads

½ teaspoon ground cardamom

freshly ground black pepper

GARNISH

fresh coriander (Chinese parsley) sprigs, red onion rings, lemon wedges, tomato wedges and baby zucchini (courgettes), blanched

TRIM the chicken and remove any excess fat. Cut the marylands in two at the joint. Halve the breasts. Pat dry with absorbent paper towels. Combine the lemon juice, salt and paprika in a glass or ceramic dish. Add the chicken pieces and marinate in the refrigerator for several hours, turning every now and then. Heat half the butter in a large, heavy frying pan and sauté the chicken in several lots (do not overcrowd the pan), until golden and tender.

MIX together the saffron, cardamom and pepper, and press onto the chicken with the back of a spoon. Sauté lightly to firm the spices onto the chicken. Add the remaining butter, heating it thoroughly and spooning over the chicken while doing so. Serve hot with naan bread or pita bread which has been brushed with butter and toasted. Garnish with the coriander sprigs, onion rings, lemon wedges, tomato wedges and zucchini.

SERVES 4–6

RIGHT: Spiced Buttery Chicken with paprika, saffron and cardamom, those most colourful of spices, served on toasted naan

PAN-FRIED CHICKEN ON GARLIC POTATO PUREE

Chicken breasts are marinated for extra flavour, then gently pan-fried in a little olive oil until golden and succulent. Served on a garlicky purée of potatoes and surrounded with a fresh-tasting tomato salsa, this dish is so simple, but so delicious.

INGREDIENTS

4 half chicken breasts or *fillets*

2 tomatoes, peeled, seeded and diced

½ cup (125 mL/4 fl oz) extra virgin olive oil

30 g (1 oz) butter

Garlic Potato Purée (see below)

freshly ground black pepper

1 tablespoon fresh snipped chives or *shredded basil*

MARINADE

juice of ½ lemon

1 clove garlic, crushed with a little salt

freshly ground black pepper

1–2 tablespoons virgin olive oil

COMBINE the marinade ingredients in a shallow glass or ceramic bowl. Add the chicken pieces and marinate for at least an hour. Place the tomatoes in a small saucepan with ¼ cup (60 mL/2 fl oz) of the olive oil and heat. Heat the remaining olive oil and the butter in a large, heavy frying pan. Add the chicken breasts, skin side down, and fry gently until golden brown, about 5–6 minutes on each side. Remove rib bones if liked. Pile potato purée onto a heated plate, top with the chicken and spoon around the tomatoes, seasoned well with a fresh grinding of pepper. Top with snipped chives or shredded basil.

SERVES 4

GARLIC POTATO PUREE

INGREDIENTS

6 medium potatoes, peeled and halved

60 g (2 oz) butter

6 cloves garlic, simmered gently in a little stock until very soft

½–1 cup (125–250 mL/4–8 fl oz) hot milk

salt and freshly ground black pepper

COOK the potatoes in boiling, salted water until soft. Drain, return to the saucepan and shake pan over a low heat until potatoes are dry. Mash, adding the butter and garlic flesh, which is squeezed out using a thumb and index finger, then mash the potatoes again. Gradually beat in enough hot milk to make the potatoes light and fluffy. Season to taste with salt and pepper.

SERVES 4

NOTE For another version of this recipe, see page 84.

GRILLED CHICKEN WITH THAI CURRY MARINADE

You can cook this dish under a conventional grill (broiler) or on an outdoor barbecue—either way is delicious. Thai curry pastes are available at most good delicatessens; some are fiery, so use with discretion.

INGREDIENTS

1 × 1.5 kg (3 lb) chicken, preferably free-range or cornfed

2 teaspoons Thai green curry paste

1 clove garlic, crushed

¼ cup (60 mL/2 fl oz) lemon juice

2 tablespoons vegetable oil

3 tablespoons thick coconut milk

salt and freshly ground pepper, to taste

WASH and dry the chicken with absorbent paper towels. Cut the chicken into four portions, trim off back bone and some of the rib cage, remove any surplus fat and place in a shallow glass or ceramic dish. Combine the curry paste, garlic, lemon juice, oil and coconut milk in a small bowl; beat well and pour over the chicken. Set aside for 15–30 minutes, turning several times.

PREHEAT the griller (broiler) and line the rack with foil. Arrange the chicken on the rack, skin side up, and brush with the curry mixture. Grill for 15 minutes, brushing frequently with the curry mixture. Turn the chicken over and brush again with the mixture. Reduce the heat, or move the chicken further away from the heat source, if it cooks too quickly. Continue grilling, brushing with the mixture until the chicken is tender, about 10–15 minutes. Grill skin side up for the last 5 minutes for a shiny, fresh finish.

SERVE with steamed rice and fresh salad vegetables, such as red onion rings, spears of Lebanese (continental) cucumber and red cherry tomatoes, and fresh coriander (Chinese parsley) sprigs.

SERVES 4

RED ONION RINGS

Red onion rings are a pretty garnish to many Oriental dishes. Cut a red onion into thin rings, drop into boiling, salted water, count to ten, then drain. Put into a small bowl and add a squeeze of lemon juice— the rings turn a pretty pink.

CHICKEN ROULADES WITH LEEKS AND MUSHROOMS

If you love having dinners at home with friends, you will know the value of something that looks spectacular, but is foolproof. Chicken breasts are rolled and tied, so they are ready for easy cooking at the last moment. Serve on a purée of potatoes or parsnip and potato purée (see page 45).

INGREDIENTS

3 whole chicken breasts, boned and with the skin left on, trimmed and dried

2 leeks, white part only, trimmed, halved and washed

45 g (1½ oz) unsalted butter

200 g (7 oz) button mushrooms, thinly sliced

⅓ cup coarsely chopped flat-leaf (Italian) parsley

1 tablespoon fresh rosemary leaves

grated rind of 1 lemon

6 thin slices prosciutto (Parma ham)

3 slices Gruyère or Emmental cheese, halved

freshly ground black pepper, to taste

½ cup (125 mL/4 fl oz) dry sherry

PLACE the chicken on a cutting surface, skin down, and remove the small fillets that are on the underside of each breast. Place a sheet of plastic wrap over each breast and pat out, as thinly as possible, using a rolling pin. Set aside. Bring a frying pan half-filled with salted water to the boil and cook the leeks for 2 minutes. Drain, cut each into 2 sections, pat dry, separate the leaves and set aside. Melt half the butter in a frying pan and sauté the mushrooms until just tender, about 5 minutes. Set aside. In a small bowl, combine the parsley, rosemary and lemon rind.

TO ASSEMBLE the chicken rolls, lay the breasts flat, skin side down. Place a slice of prosciutto on each side of the breasts. Divide the leek leaves lengthwise evenly among the breasts, and arrange the sautéed mushrooms down the centre of each breast. Sprinkle with the herb mixture and top each with 2 cheese halves. Season liberally with pepper. Starting with a long edge, roll the breasts as tightly as possible and tie neatly with string. Refrigerate until ready to cook.

PREHEAT the oven to 180°C (350°F). Melt the remaining butter in a heavy flameproof baking dish and, when sizzling, add the chicken rolls and brown for a few minutes all over. Pour in the dry sherry and continue cooking the chicken in the oven for about 20 minutes, basting frequently.

TO SERVE, remove from the oven and leave to set for about 5 minutes before removing the string. Slice the rolls into 2 cm (5 in) thick slices and arrange on dinner plates, spooning the baking juices over them.

SERVES 6

RIGHT: Chicken Roulades with Leeks and Mushrooms. A special occasion dish.

SAUTEED CHICKEN

For sauté dishes, chicken breasts may be cut from a whole chicken, the rib cage trimmed, skin left on and then cooked on the bone or as purchased skinless, boneless half-breasts and thighs of chicken. These are so quick and easy to sauté and can be served with buttered noodles or rice.

INGREDIENTS

4 chicken fillets (breasts or thighs) or ½ breasts on the bone

3 tablespoons plain (all-purpose) flour, seasoned with a little salt and freshly ground black pepper

1 tablespoon butter

1 tablespoon oil

TRIM off any jagged edges from the chicken joints. Cut and pull out the white tendon that runs down the underside of the meat. Put the seasoned flour on a piece of greaseproof (wax) paper and turn the chicken about in it until lightly coated with flour. Heat the butter and oil in a frying pan until foaming, pat the chicken to remove excess flour and place it in the pan. Sauté skin side down, if skin is on chicken, over a medium heat until golden brown, about 4 minutes. Turn and cook the other side, also about 4 minutes. Do not crowd the pan. Serve immediately, or keep warm for a minute or two while making the sauce.

SERVES 4

TESTING CHICKEN

To check when the chicken is done, press it with your finger; if it feels springy, it is ready. If still soft and yielding, cook it for a minute or two more, but keep checking. If cooked until there is no springiness, it is overdone and will be tough and dry.

CHICKEN SAUTE WITH BRANDY CREAM SAUCE
Sauté the chicken joints as above and remove to a warm dish. Pour ¼ cup (60 mL/2 fl oz) brandy or cognac into the pan and heat, stirring to collect all the brown bits from the bottom. Swirl in 4 tablespoons thick (double, whipping) cream and boil, stirring for a minute. Taste, season and spoon over the chicken.

CHICKEN SAUTE WITH LEMON AND CAPER SAUCE Sauté the chicken joints as above and remove to a warm dish. Add a piece of butter, about the size of a walnut, to the pan. Heat until foaming, stirring to collect the brown bits from the bottom, then stir in 2 tablespoons lemon juice, 1 tablespoon chopped fresh parsley and 2 teaspoons capers. Season to taste with salt and pepper, and spoon over the chicken.

CHICKEN SAUTE WITH WOOD MUSHROOM SAUCE
Sauté the chicken joints as above and remove to a warm dish. Add a piece of butter, about the size of a walnut, to the pan. Heat until foaming, put in 6–8 sliced shiitake, Swiss browns or slippery jack mushrooms and sauté the slices briskly for a minute or two, shaking the pan well. Add ⅓ cup (90 mL/3 fl oz) fresh (single, light) cream and

boil, stirring, for a minute, then stir in 1 tablespoon sherry or brandy. Taste, correct seasoning and spoon over the chicken. If wood or shiitake mushrooms are not available, use white button mushrooms.

WILD OR WOOD MUSHROOMS

These mushrooms have an earthy, robust, rich texture and flavour. They make the most interesting mushroom sauces. Swiss browns and slippery jacks are close to wild wood mushrooms. Look also for shiitake, Roman brown and flat field mushrooms.

CHICKEN VERONIQUE This is the name given to chicken or fish with grapes. Sauté the chicken joints as above and remove to a warm dish. Swirl in a piece of butter about the size of a walnut, heat until foaming, add ½ cup (125 mL/4 fl oz) white wine, stirring to collect the brown bits from the bottom of the pan. Add 1 cup seeded fresh grapes. For a creamy finish, 2–3 tablespoons fresh (single, light) cream may be added; bring to the boil, then spoon over the chicken.

DEVILLED SPATCHCOCK

Small young chickens are grilled, then topped with devilled breadcrumbs and further grilled.

INGREDIENTS

2 small spatchcocks or poussins,
  about 500 g (1 lb)
15 g (½ oz) butter, softened
salt

DEVIL MIXTURE

30 g (1 oz) butter, softened
1 teaspoon dry English mustard
pinch of cayenne pepper
1 teaspoon Worcestershire sauce
1 cup (60 g/2 oz) fresh breadcrumbs

GRILLING CHICKEN

This is a good method of cooking the smallest and youngest chickens or spatchcock. As they are too young to have put on much flesh and developed much flavour, they need butter to keep moist and add flavour. Best eaten with your fingers.

SPLIT the chickens down the back, cut into halves if liked, clean and dry well. Spread the skin with butter and sprinkle it with salt. Preheat the grill or broiler—gas or electric—for about 10 minutes, and brush the rack with oil or butter.

TO MAKE the Devil Mixture, cream the softened butter with the mustard, cayenne and Worcestershire sauce, then mix with the breadcrumbs. Set aside.

COOK the birds on the rack, about 10 cm (4 in) from the heat and with the skin side facing the heat, until the skin is a rich golden brown, about 15 minutes. Turn and brush with butter or drippings, and cook for a further 10 minutes. Turn the chicken again. Sprinkle skin side with the devil mixture and continue to grill until golden. Keep the heat low enough so that the crumbs do not brown too much, but have a nice golden colour. Lift off carefully to keep the crust intact.

SERVE hot with a fresh green salad and crusty or flat bread to mop up the juices.

SERVES 2

BEDOUIN COUSCOUS WITH CHICKEN AND VEGETABLES

A holiday in Morocco introduced me to the joys of a lavish meal of couscous, Bedouin style. Replete with spices, a myriad of colourful vegetables, golden saffron-hued chicken or succulent lamb, plump raisins and fiery harissa, I quickly developed a predilection for this Moroccan speciality, so perfect for informal entertaining.

INGREDIENTS

500 g (1 lb) couscous

90 g (3 oz) butter

2 cloves garlic, crushed

¼ teaspoon saffron threads

1 teaspoon ground cumin

1 teaspoon ground turmeric

½ teaspoon ground ginger

2 tablespoons tomato paste

salt and freshly ground black pepper

1 × 1.5 kg (3 lb) chicken, cut into joints

3 medium carrots, peeled and cut into sticks

500 g (1 lb) pumpkin, peeled and cut into cubes

2 large tomatoes, peeled, quartered and seeded

4 zucchini (courgettes), cut the same size as the carrots

1 × 435 g (14 oz) can chickpeas (garbanzo beans)

a little stock or butter

2 tablespoons raisins (optional)

harissa sauce, to serve

preserved lemon, to serve

COVER the couscous with cold water, stir with the fingers and drain. Stand 15 minutes to allow couscous to swell. Repeat this process once more.

TO COOK the chicken, melt half the butter in a large, heavy saucepan, add the garlic, saffron, cumin, turmeric, ginger, bay leaf and tomato paste. Season to taste with salt and pepper. Stir well and add the chicken pieces; cook until golden, then add the carrots, pumpkin and tomatoes. Add just enough water to cover and bring to the boil. Place the swollen couscous in a colander lined with a fine tea towel (cloth) which will fit snugly into the top of the pan. Place over the vegetables, cover well and simmer gently for about 40 minutes. The couscous grains should not touch the liquid. After 20 minutes, add the remaining butter to the couscous and the zucchini to the chicken and vegetables. Fluff up the couscous occasionally with a fork during the cooking. Heat the chickpeas in a little stock or butter, add the raisins (if using) and fold through the couscous.

TO SERVE, pile the couscous onto a large heated platter, make a well in the centre and pile the chicken and vegetables into the centre and around the couscous. Serve immediately with a small bowl of harissa and some pieces of preserved lemon for a hot and tart finish.

SERVES 6

LEFT: Couscous with Chicken and Vegetables Bedouin Style served with harissa, the fiery Moroccan paste, and preserved lemon

QUAIL WITH GRAPES

These little birds are delectable treated this way and are best eaten with your fingers, so be sure to provide finger bowls.

INGREDIENTS

6–8 quail
salt and freshly ground black pepper
1–2 teaspoons chopped fresh mint leaves
60 g (2 oz) unsalted butter
1 cup (250 mL/8 fl oz) freshly pressed white grape juice
1 cup (185 g/6 oz) seedless grapes

PAT dry the quail and season them with the salt, pepper and mint. In a large, heavy frying pan, melt the butter over a moderately high heat until foaming. Add the quail and cook for 3–4 minutes on each side, or until the juices run clear when the thighs are pierced with a skewer. Transfer the birds to a warm serving plate and keep warm while making the gravy. If your frying pan is not large enough, you may have to add more butter and cook the quail in two lots.

POUR off any excess butter from the pan, add the grape juice and stir over a moderately high heat, scraping up any brown bits. When reduced and syrupy, heat the grapes in the sauce then spoon over the quail. If liked, serve with a small mound of steamed wild rice or long-grain rice, or a combination of both.

SERVES 4

WILD AND LONG-GRAIN RICE

This combination of wild and white rice is a perfect accompaniment for game, turkey, goose and quail.

INGREDIENTS

¾ cup (125 g/4 oz) long-grain white rice
¾ cup (155 g/5 oz) wild rice
salt and freshly ground black pepper
2–3 teaspoons butter

RINSE the long-grain and the wild rice separately in a sieve under cold running water, until the water runs clear. To cook the long-grain rice, bring 1½ cups (375 mL/12 fl oz) water to the boil in a heavy saucepan with ½ teaspoon salt. Sprinkle in the rice through your fingers so that the water does not go off the boil. Stir once, then cover with a well-fitting lid and reduce the heat to very low. Do not lift the lid until the last few minutes of cooking. Cook very gently for 10–15 minutes, or until a test grain is tender, but still firm when bitten. Remove from the heat and fluff up lightly with a fork. For very dry, fluffy grains, set the rice aside, still covered, for 5 minutes before fluffing up.

TO COOK the wild rice, cover the rice with cold, salted water in a heavy saucepan. Bring to the boil, skim any foreign particles from the top and drain. Bring 3 cups (750 mL/24 fl oz) fresh water to the boil, add 1 teaspoon salt and stir in the rice slowly. Cook without stirring for about 30 minutes, or until the grains are tender, adding a little more boiling water if necessary. Fluff up with a fork.

TO COMBINE, toss the cooked white rice and wild rice together, add the butter and a grinding of pepper.

MAKES ABOUT 4 ½ CUPS

ROAST DUCK WITH MANGO SALSA

The mango and chilli salsa flecked with mint goes beautifully with the duck.

INGREDIENTS

2 young ducklings
salt and freshly ground pepper
45 g (1½ oz) butter
Wild and Long-Grain Rice
1 quantity Mango Chilli Salsa
sprigs of fresh mint, to serve

PREHEAT the oven to 260°C (500°F). Split the ducks into halves using poultry scissors and a strong knife, removing all the noticeable fat. Season the duck with salt and pepper, and place skin side up on a rack in a roasting pan. Roast for 10 minutes to render some of the fat from under the skin, then let the duck cool. Reduce the oven to 180°C (350°F) and return the duck to the oven. Continue cooking for about 30 minutes, until tender, or done to taste. Set aside in a warm place while finishing off rice and salsa.

TO CRISP the duck skin, place the duck skin side up under a hot grill (broiler), just long enough to heat the duck and crisp the skin. Remove the whole legs from the duck and slice the breasts slightly diagonally across. Place the legs and fanned slices of breast on 4 warm serving plates. Serve the rice alongside and spoon on some Mango Chilli Salsa. Garnish with mint sprigs.

SERVES 4

DUCK BREASTS WITH BLUEBERRY AND BALSAMIC SAUCE

This recipe is for people who have noticed duck breasts are available in speciality food halls and game suppliers. It is a delicious recipe for special occasions such as Easter or birthday dinners. The French and most gourmets like duck breast pink.

INGREDIENTS

4 duck breasts

1–2 tablespoons light olive oil

1 tablespoon red wine vinegar

good pinch of sugar

¼ teaspoon ground cinnamon

salt and freshly ground black pepper

4 tablespoons blueberries or
*   raspberries*

1 tablespoon balsamic vinegar

CUTTING A DUCK

A whole young duckling may be cut into four—2 breasts and 2 hind quarters with legs—trimmed and treated the same way; allow an extra 15 minutes cooking for legs.

RIGHT: Duck Breasts with Blueberry and Balsamic Sauce is equally good with the tart–sweet taste of raspberries

TRIM the back bone and breast bones from the duck breasts. Heat the oil in a large frying pan. Gently fry the duck breasts skin side down, until skin is golden. Turn and add the red wine vinegar, sugar and cinnamon. Season with salt and pepper. Cover and cook gently for 10 minutes until the duck breasts are tender and still juicy inside. Add 3 tablespoons berries and continue cooking for 5 minutes, or until the berries have melted into a delicious sauce. Lastly, swirl in the balsamic vinegar, let it bubble for a few seconds and check the sauce for seasoning. Just before serving, add the remaining berries and heat through.

SERVE the duck breasts cut into thick slices on a bed of Garlic Potato Purée (see page 96) with the sauce poured over the top. Serve a green vegetable of your choice—asparagus, green peas, baby beans, baby turnips or beetroot.

SERVES 4

GRILLED DUCK BREAST is simply delicious. As the duck breast is often fatty, the skin is scored in several places; the fat runs off during grilling. Rub the skin with a little freshly ground pepper and sea salt. Place the breasts skin-side up under a preheated grill (broiler) and grill for 8–10 minutes; pour off excess fat as it gathers, to prevent it catching alight. Turn breasts and cook for a further 2–3 minutes. Transfer to a hot platter, cover loosely with foil and stand in a warm place for 5 minutes. Serve with a green salad and Mango Chilli Salsa (see page 105).

CHAPTER 8

THE NOBLE MEATS

It is no chore to become familiar with all the meats, the cuts of each, and care about how they will be cooked and turned into special dishes that will be the basis of a convivial meal. Spices are used as flavouring for lamb, as are herbs such as oregano and rosemary. The English love roast lamb with mint sauce; the Moroccans prefer it with cumin and salt; the French with garlic. Beef is always held in high esteem—the most tender cuts are prized for grilling and roasting, the flavoursome tougher cuts for long, slow cooking. Pork is appreciated for its versatility.

VEAL WITH WHITE WINE AND SAGE

Veal can readily take the addition of robust flavours to enhance its delicate taste. In this Italian dish, sage provides the answer; the wine also adds its own distinctive flavour and character.

INGREDIENTS

750 g (1½ lb) lean veal cubes, cut
    from shoulder
plain (all-purpose) flour, seasoned
    with salt and freshly ground black
    pepper, for dusting
45 g (1½ oz) butter
1 cup (250 mL/8 fl oz) dry
    white wine
8 fresh sage leaves, roughly chopped
¼ cup (60 mL/2 fl oz) stock or water

DUST the veal lightly with the seasoned flour. Heat the butter in a large sauté pan and, when sizzling, add the veal and sauté over a moderate heat until golden. You may need to do this in two batches.
ADD the wine and allow to bubble briskly for a minute before adding the sage. Reduce the heat, half-cover the pan with a lid and simmer gently for about 50 minutes, until the veal is tender. Add a little stock or water if necessary during cooking to keep the dish moist. Serve hot with rice or noodles, or boiled or creamy mashed potatoes. Offer a crisp green salad to follow, served on the same plate—the gravy adds flavour to the salad, a very French idea.
SERVES 4

VEAL SCALOPPINE

The intense flavour of aged balsamic vinegar is used sparingly for a superb finish.

INGREDIENTS

4 large or *8 small veal scaloppine, pounded very thin and trimmed*

plain (all-purpose) flour, seasoned with salt and black pepper

1 tablespoon extra virgin olive oil

½ cup (125 mL/4 fl oz) chicken stock or *white wine*

1 tablespoon butter

1 tablespoon balsamic vinegar

1 tablespoon capers

salt and freshly ground pepper

¼ cup (125 g/4 oz) chopped parsley

CUT the veal scaloppine in two if large. Place the seasoned flour on a sheet of kitchen paper and lightly dust the veal with the flour. In a large frying pan, heat the oil over a moderately high heat and brown the veal for about 2 minutes on each side, doing so in several lots. Remove from the pan and place on a heated serving platter.

RETURN the pan to the heat and add the chicken stock or wine. Over a moderate heat, allow the liquid to reduce slightly, scraping up any brown bits from the pan. Reduce the heat, and stir in the butter, vinegar and capers to heat through. Season with a little salt and pepper, and spoon the sauce from the pan over the scaloppine. Sprinkle with freshly chopped parsley. Rice, noodles or sautéed potatoes go well with this dish.

SERVES 4

VEAL CHOPS WITH TARRAGON

Veal chops are lightly sautéed in butter and then simmered gently in wine flavoured with tarragon.

INGREDIENTS

6 thick veal rib cutlets

3 tablespoons plain (all-purpose) flour

2 tablespoons butter

2 tablespoons olive oil

salt and freshly ground black pepper

2 tablespoons chopped golden shallots

½ cup (125 mL/4 fl oz) dry white wine, such as Chardonnay

2 teaspoons chopped fresh tarragon

½ cup (125 mL/4 fl oz) fresh (single, light) cream

PREHEAT the oven to 180°C (350°F). Dust the veal with the flour, shaking off any excess. Heat the butter and oil in a heavy frying pan and brown the veal for 3–4 minutes on each side. Season with salt and pepper, and arrange in a single layer in a flameproof casserole. Add the shallots to the frying pan in which the cutlets were browned and cook gently for 5 minutes. Add the wine and tarragon, and simmer for 3 minutes. Pour over the cutlets, cover and bake in the oven for 20 minutes or until the cutlets are tender. Lift out the veal and place on a heated serving dish. Add the cream to the dish and stir over a gentle heat until heated through. Pour over the veal and serve.

SERVES 4–6

BEEF AND PRUNE CASSEROLE

The French cook many meat dishes with fruit—a few prunes are added here to give a rich gravy.

INGREDIENTS

2½ cups (625mL/1 imp. pint) beef stock (page 12)

8 prunes or black pickled walnuts

1 kg (2 lb) chuck or blade bone steak, cut thick

2 tablespoons plain (all-purpose) flour, seasoned with salt and freshly ground black pepper

60 g (2 oz) butter

1 tablespoon olive oil

1 tablespoon tomato paste

2 bay leaves

2 ripe red tomatoes, skinned, quartered and seeded

HEAT the stock and pour over the prunes in a bowl. Soak for about 30 minutes. Cut the steak into 5 cm (2 in.) cubes and roll in the seasoned flour. Heat the butter and oil in a large, deep-sided frying pan or casserole dish and brown the meat all over.

STRAIN the stock from the prunes and add to the meat. Bring to the boil and cook for a few minutes. Add the tomato paste, 2 finely chopped prunes or walnuts, and bay leaves. Cover and simmer for 1¾ hours. Add the remaining prunes or walnuts, and the tomatoes. Cook for a further 15 minutes. Serve with a generous sprinkling of parsley, if liked. Offer with a dish of creamy mashed potatoes or quartered steamed potatoes, or crusty French bread to mop up the delicious gravy.

SERVES 6

VEAL CHOPS WITH BASIL BUTTER

INGREDIENTS

2 tablespoons olive oil

6–8 rib veal chops, trimmed or 'frenched' as for lamb cutlets

BASIL BUTTER

60 g (2 oz) unsalted butter

1 teaspoon grated lemon rind

1 golden shallot, chopped

2 tablespoons chopped basil leaves

salt and freshly ground pepper

RIGHT: Beef and Prune Casserole, a timeless classic

CREAM the butter in a small bowl and beat in the lemon rind, then the shallot, basil and salt and pepper to taste. Shape into a roll and wrap in a piece of foil. Chill until firm—this may take an hour and can be done well in advance.

HEAT a ribbed grill pan or grill (broiler), and brush with the olive oil. Pat the veal chops dry and season with salt and pepper. Cook with a moderately high heat for 5 minutes on each side, until golden and still slightly pink inside. Top each veal chop with one or two thin slices of the basil butter. Serve with creamy mashed potatoes or sautéed potatoes, and follow with a green salad.

SERVES 3–4

ROAST FILLET OF BEEF

Fillet of beef is rightly considered the finest cut of this meat. It is often cooked whole. For a dinner party, serve it sliced, at room temperature, with a good sauce. Many people choose béarnaise, the queen of rich, buttery sauces, or a green herb sauce. Alternatively, you can pick up the pan juices with a little Madeira or white wine, or even a good stock.

INGREDIENTS

1.5 kg (3 lb) fillet of beef
(tenderloin), trimmed and tied
(below)
freshly ground black pepper
1 tablespoon olive oil
30 g (1 oz) butter
3 tablespoons brandy

PAN GRAVY

¾ cup (185 mL/6 fl oz) Madeira or
wine or stock
2 teaspoons butter
salt and freshly ground black pepper

To Trim Fillet of Beef
Remove surface fat and membrane covering the meat with a sharp knife. You can leave a little fat on to add extra flavour. After trimming, tie the fillet neatly with string at regular intervals, so that it keeps its shape during cooking.

SEASON the fillet with the pepper. Preheat the oven to 260°C (500°F). Heat the oil in a flameproof baking dish (roasting pan), then add the butter. When hot, add the beef and brown well all over. Heat the brandy, set it alight and pour it over the beef. Shake the pan until the flames subside. Place the pan in the oven and turn the heat down to 220°C (425°F). Cook for 15–20 minutes.

REMOVE the beef and allow it to rest, covered loosely in foil, for 10–15 minutes. Make the gravy. Remove the string and carve the meat into 1 cm (½ in.) slices. Arrange on a serving dish and brush with a little of the gravy to keep the meat moist. To serve, spoon a little of the gravy on each plate, top with a few slices of the fillet and serve with lightly cooked green beans and steamed baby potatoes or Garlic Purée Potatoes (page 96).

SERVES 6–8

TO MAKE PAN GRAVY
Put the baking dish over a moderate heat. Add the Madeira or white wine or stock. Simmer, stirring in the brown bits from the pan. Swirl the butter around the pan. Season with salt and pepper to taste. Put the gravy into a small jug or gravy boat to serve.

GREEN SAUCE This is the lovely pungent green sauce of Italy. It often accompanies the boiled meats of Florence, cold fish or a fillet of beef. Place 1 cup parsley sprigs, 8 small pickled gherkins, 3 tablespoons capers, 6–8 anchovy fillets, 1 tablespoon green peppercorns and the grated rind of 1 lemon in an electric blender or food processor. Purée until a smooth paste, working in ⅔ cup (170 mL/5½ fl oz) olive oil. Alternatively, pound the mixture using a mortar and pestle.

PORK WITH BEAN SPROUTS AND CHIVES

Most of us have that wonder of utensils—a wok—and enjoy using it for quick and delicious meals; this one takes all of 5 minutes! The flat garlic chives are a great delicacy when cooked lightly and are a contrast to the crunchy, nutty sprouts.

INGREDIENTS

2 tablespoons vegetable oil

2 cloves garlic, crushed

250 g (8 oz) pork fillet, finely sliced

250 g (8 oz) bean sprouts, ends
  trimmed

100 g (3½ oz) Chinese garlic chives

1 tablespoon fish sauce (nam pla)

1 teaspoon sugar

freshly ground white peppercorns

½ cup torn fresh coriander (Chinese
  parsley) leaves

HEAT the oil in the wok, add the garlic and sauté until fragrant; do not allow to brown. Add the sliced pork and continue to stir-fry until the meat is cooked, about 3 minutes. Toss in the bean sprouts, chives, fish sauce and sugar. Cook for about 1 minute, or until heated through. Serve sprinkled with the pepper and coriander. Accompany with steamed rice.

SERVES 4

PORK CHOPS WITH SAGE AND ONION

INGREDIENTS

4–6 thick pork chops, rind and
  excess fat removed

1 cup (60 g/2 oz) day-old bread
  cubes

½ small onion, finely chopped

1 tablespoon olive oil

1 apple, grated

1 tablespoon chopped fresh parsley

6 sage leaves, slivered

salt and freshly ground pepper

1 red-skinned apple

1 tablespoon honey

grated nutmeg

¼ cup (60 mL/2 fl oz) hot water

PREHEAT the oven to 180°C (350°F). Slit chops from the outer edge to the bone to make a pocket. Combine the bread cubes, onion, oil, apple, parsley, sage, salt and pepper in a bowl. Mix well with a fork. Stuff the chops and secure openings with wooden toothpicks. Put in a shallow casserole. Bake in the oven until well browned, about 20 minutes. Cut the apple into 4–6 slices and arrange on each chop. Brush with the honey and sprinkle with nutmeg. Add the hot water, cover and bake until chops are tender and apple glazed, about 45 minutes. Serve with a green salad.

SERVES 4–6

NOTE I like to cut pockets in the pork chops and stuff them with breadcrumbs, onions, grated apple and sage.

CHARGRILLED LAMB WITH APPLE AND SAFFRON CHUTNEY

Best end of lamb cutlets, prepared from the forequarter, are a treat and may be cooked over glowing coals, under a grill or on a ribbed grill.

INGREDIENTS

4 lamb racks of 4 cutlets each, from forequarter
salt and freshly ground black pepper
olive oil
Apple and Saffron Chutney (below)

SEASON the lamb with salt and pepper, and a drizzle of olive oil. Place on a rack. Preheat the grill or broiler. Cook the lamb, turning several times, for 10–12 minutes. (You can also use a ribbed grill to cook the lamb.) Rest the lamb for at least 5 minutes before serving. Serve with the Apple and Saffron Chutney, creamy mashed potatoes and a salad.

SERVES 4

APPLE AND SAFFRON CHUTNEY

A fresh-tasting chutney adds interest to grilled and barbecued meats. It is equally good with cold meats.

INGREDIENTS

pinch of saffron threads
¼ cup (60 mL/2 fl oz) white wine
2 tablespoons sugar
2 tablespoons white wine vinegar
1 tablespoon Chinese plum sauce
1 bird's eye red chilli
piece of star anise
stick of cinnamon
3 Fuji or other crisp apples, peeled, cored and diced
3 tablespoons raisins
2 tablespoons toasted pine nuts

IN A bowl, mix the saffron, wine, sugar, vinegar, plum sauce, red chilli, star anise and cinnamon. Put the saffron mixture in a heavy saucepan and bring slowly to the boil. Cook until the liquid has reduced a little. Add the apples, raisins and pine nuts, and cook gently, stirring occasionally. The chutney is ready when the apples are soft. Remove the star anise, cinnamon stick and chilli before serving if preferred.

PEACH AND SAFFRON CHUTNEY Make as above, but cut 3 firm, peeled yellow peaches into dice and proceed with recipe. Mango chutney may be made the same way using the flesh of 3 firm mangoes.

LEFT: Chargrilled Lamb with Apple and Saffron Chutney—timing is everything when cooking this dish

SHOULDER OF LAMB WITH TWO HEADS OF GARLIC

I like this long, slow way of cooking a shoulder of lamb on the bone. Carving can be difficult, but the meat is so tender I pull it away in large pieces. The drippings from lamb give a delicious flavour to potatoes baked at the bottom of the dish. The anchovies, garlic and vinegar do wonders, as does the long, slow cooking.

INGREDIENTS

1.75–2 kg (3¾–4½ lb) shoulder
of lamb
salt and freshly ground black pepper
1½ tablespoons light olive oil
30 g (1 oz) unsalted butter
1 kg (2 lb) potatoes, peeled and
thinly sliced
2 medium onions, halved and sliced
4 anchovy fillets
2 heads of garlic
fresh rosemary sprig, broken into
small sprigs
1½ tablespoons white wine vinegar
2 cups (500 mL/16 fl oz) water

PREHEAT the oven to 180°C (350°F). Trim any excess fat from the lamb. Rub the lamb with salt and pepper. Heat a heavy, flameproof baking dish (roasting pan) over a moderately high heat. Add the lamb and brown all over, turning frequently, until well browned. Lift out of the pan onto a plate.

SPREAD the potatoes and onions in layers on the bottom of the baking dish. Dot with the anchovy fillets, sprinkling each one with a layer of salt and a small amount of pepper. Remove any excess layers of papery skin from the garlic, cut the garlic heads in half across, and place in the potatoes. Lay the lamb on top of the the potato mixture. Sprinkle the rosemary and vinegar over the whole dish, and pour the water over the potatoes. Cover with foil and bake in the oven for 3 hours, taking the foil off after 1½ hours and reducing the heat to 160°C (325°F).

TO SERVE, transfer the lamb to a hot platter and the vegetables to a separate warmed platter. Cut the meat off in chunky pieces—it will almost fall apart. Each guest gets half a garlic head, from which they will scoop out the tender flesh to season the lamb. Serve accompanied by the potatoes. This is good followed by a crisp green salad.

SERVES 4

TENDER LAMB

Look for very young lamb for this dish—its wonderful sweet, succulent and meltingly tender texture is the result of slow cooking. Older lamb is still good, but results in a more robust dish.

LAMB AND CAULIFLOWER MA GOSH

A lamb and cauliflower combination cooked gently in spices and coconut milk—which is available canned, in cartons or in solid packs—makes a lovely curry meal served with steamed aromatic rice.

INGREDIENTS

500 g (1 lb) boneless leg of lamb

4 tablespoons melted ghee or vegetable oil

2 onions, sliced

4 cloves garlic, crushed

2.5 cm (1 in.) piece of fresh ginger, grated

5 cm (2 in.) stick cinnamon

1 whole dried chilli

1 cup (250 mL/8 fl oz) water

1 teaspoon salt

1 medium cauliflower, cut into small florets

2 cups (500 mL/16 fl oz) canned coconut milk or ½ cup (125 mL/ 4 fl oz) coconut cream and ½ cup (125 mL/4 fl oz) water, combined

TRIM the lamb of any excess fat and cut into small cubes. Set aside. Heat the ghee or oil in large, heavy saucepan or Dutch oven. Add the onions and sauté until golden. Pour off any excess oil. Add the garlic and ginger, and cook gently for a few minutes. Add the meat and brown, adding a little more ghee or oil if necessary. Add the cinnamon stick, chilli, water and salt. Cover and cook over a low heat until the meat is cooked and only a little of the gravy remains.

ADD the coconut milk, or combined coconut cream and water, and the cauliflower. Blend well, cover and cook over a low heat until the cauliflower is cooked and only about ¾ cup (185 mL/6 fl oz) thick gravy remains. Remove the chilli. Serve with Steamed Aromatic Rice.

SERVES 6

STEAMED AROMATIC RICE In a heavy saucepan, put 2 cups (500 mL/16 fl oz) chicken stock, 1 whole onion, 4 whole cardamon pods, 1 stick cinnamon and 1 bay leaf. Bring to the boil and add 1 cup (155 g/5 oz) washed jasmine or basmati rice; stir well. Bring to a simmer, cook for 5 minutes, cover, and cook for a further 15 minutes. Remove onion and, if liked, the whole spices. Fluff up rice with a fork. You can serve this rice with most Indian or western meals.

BASMATI AND JASMINE RICE

Basmati rice is from Pakistan. It is a light-textured long-grain rice with a wonderful aromatic flavour. Jasmine rice from Southeast Asia is a lightly perfumed long-grain rice. Both rices, which are not brand names but varieties, go well with all types of Asian cuisine.

RACK OF LAMB WITH CUMIN AND THYME

Everyone enjoys a rack of lamb. Here it is served in the simplest, but best of all possible ways. I've allowed 3 cutlets per person, but with small young spring lamb, someone might enjoy an extra cutlet. Serve with sauté potatoes, steamed new potatoes or oven-roasted kipfler potatoes, and a green salad to follow. If liked, offer a fruit chutney perhaps Peach and Saffron Chutney (see page 115).

INGREDIENTS

2 racks of lamb, consisting of
  6–7 cutlets each
30 g (1 oz) butter
1 teaspoon lemon thyme leaves
1 teaspoon ground cumin
½ teaspoon salt
freshly ground black pepper, to taste
grated rind of 1 lemon
1 tablespoon lemon juice
1½ cups (90 g/3 oz) fresh
  breadcrumbs
1 tablespoon Dijon mustard

PREHEAT the oven to 220°C (425°F). Trim the cutlets (if your butcher has not done so) by cutting away the flesh from the top of the bone and slicing the fat away, leaving about 5 cm (2 in.) of the bone exposed. Cut off any excess fat. Score the lamb with shallow diagonal cuts in a lattice fashion using a sharp knife. Heat a large frying pan and sear the meat over a low heat for 4–5 minutes or until golden all over. Leave to cool to room temperature.

MAKE the crusty topping. Melt the butter and mix with the lemon thyme, cumin, salt, pepper, lemon rind and juice, and breadcrumbs in a bowl. Toss together lightly. Spread the lamb with the mustard and then top with a thick, compact layer of breadcrumb mixture.

PLACE the lamb in a baking dish and roast the oven for 10 minutes. When the lamb is cooked, the juices will run clear. Allow to stand for a few minutes. Cut each rack into serving slices, allowing two or three cutlets per person.

SERVES 4

Right: Rack of Lamb with Cumin and Thyme. The lamb is pan-fried and then left to cool. It is then topped with the crumbs and roasted just as it is required, for only 10 minutes. This is very convenient, especially when entertaining

LAMB TENDERLOIN WITH SUMMER VEGETABLES

A whole tenderloin is cooked in a heavy frying pan. It is important to rest the meat before cutting and while the vegetables are finished off at the last moment. A very contemporary dish that takes advantage of prime lamb and tender baby vegetables.

INGREDIENTS

1 lamb eye of loin, trimmed

2 sprigs fresh rosemary

sea salt and freshly ground pepper

2 tablespoons olive oil

¾ cup (185 mL/6 fl oz) lamb or beef stock

2 red capsicum (sweet peppers)

2 fresh corn cobs

4 finger-length eggplants (aubergines)

4 medium zucchini (courgettes)

8 yellow baby button squash

1 tablespoon chopped flat-leaf (Italian) parsley

EYE OF LOIN

To understand trim lamb eye of loin, visualise a loin chop. On one side of the bone is a small tender piece of meat known as the fillet (this is also called tenderloin). On the other side of the bone is a larger piece of meat called the eye loin (also known as the backstrap). By removing the bone and fat from the whole loin the fillet and eye of loin are left in a single whole piece.

SPRINKLE the lamb with the rosemary leaves and salt, and season generously with pepper. Heat the olive oil in a large heavy frying pan, and when hot, add the lamb and brown all over, turning frequently, for about 8 minutes. Test for doneness. Remove the lamb from the pan and allow to stand, wrapped loosely in foil, for 10–15 minutes. Deglaze the pan with the stock, cooking until the liquid is reduced by half. Set aside and keep warm.

PLACE the capsicums under a hot grill (broiler) and grill until charred and blackened. Place in a brown paper bag and allow to steam for a few minutes. Rinse under cold water and scrape the charred skin off with a sharp knife. Halve the capsicums, remove the core and seeds, and cut into 2.5 cm (1 in.) pieces.

REMOVE the husks and silk tassels from the corn and cut lengthwise from the top down to remove the kernels. Boil the corn in a saucepan of water for 4–6 minutes until tender. Drain. Meanwhile, cut the eggplant, zucchini and squash into squares of similar size. Gently stir-fry the vegetables in a little olive oil, until they are cooked, but still crunchy. Add the corn and toss through with the chopped parsley. Season with salt and pepper. To serve, divide the corn and vegetable mixture among 4 warmed plates. Cut the lamb into cubes and arrange on top. Spoon the reduced stock over each portion and serve.

SERVES 4

CHAPTER 9

FISH AND SEAFOOD

I have always loved fish and shellfish. It is no coincidence that
I now live close to the sea and one of the best fish markets in the world.
Tiny sardines, octopus, crates of wriggling crayfish, rosy red mounds of
those crabs that have already hit the pot, plus bags of oysters smelling of
the sea and much-prized sashimi tuna. How to choose?
One word of warning, it is a crime to overcook fish.

GRILLED FISH WITH GINGER

*The lovely wild fish—blue eye cod, salmon, snapper, barramundi—
are like most fish, at their best when simply grilled.*

INGREDIENTS

*8 slices green ginger, cut into fine
   'needles'*

2 tablespoons light olive oil

*1 tablespoon rice wine or rice
   vinegar*

2 teaspoons soy sauce

pinch of sugar

pinch of freshly ground black pepper

*2 tablespoons dry white wine or
   water*

*4 large, thick, fish fillets or cutlets
   of any good white fish, wiped*

COMBINE all the ingredients except the fish in a flat glass or ceramic dish. Add the fish and marinate for 5–10 minutes, turning halfway through. Slash the skin through the thickest part of the fillet for even cooking.

PREHEAT the grill (broiler), including a flat tray underneath lined with foil. Place the fish on it skin-side up. Spoon over half the marinade and grill at the hottest heat, about 2–4 minutes depending on thickness, or until the fish has turned white and opaque. Spoon over the remaining marinade, turn the cutlets (fillets don't need to be turned) and continue grilling until the fish is cooked, another 2–3 minutes. Transfer the fish to a heated platter and spoon over any marinade remaining in the pan. Serve with mesclun or a green leaf salad and steamed potatoes.

SERVES 4

LAKSA LEMAK

Laksa Lemak, from central Indonesia and Malaysia, is the best known of laksas. For a feast, go all the way with the garnishes or, if you prefer, select just a few. What makes this exotic, time-consuming dish simpler to make and yet authentic is using one of the excellent laksa pastes on the market. You can make the paste yourself; I have included the recipe.

STOCK

500 g (1 lb) green medium king
  prawns (shrimp), with shells
2 cups (500 mL/16 fl oz) water

LAKSA

2 tablespoons oil
2–3 tablespoons laksa paste
4 cups (1 litre/1¾ imp. pints) thin
  coconut milk
1 cup (250 mL/8 fl oz) thick
  coconut milk (cream)

GARNISHES

125 g (4 oz) fish pieces (optional)
tofu (bean curd), cubed
6 shiitake mushrooms, soaked,
  stems removed and shredded
500 g (1 lb) fresh laksa noodles or
  rice-flour noodles, soaked in
  boiling water for 3 minutes,
  drained and kept warm
6–8 crisp-fried brown shallots
2 boiled eggs, quartered
1 cup bean sprouts, ends trimmed
2 limes, quartered
1 fresh chilli, sliced
fresh Thai or Vietnamese mint (ram
  rau) sprigs

TO MAKE the stock, shell the prawns and devein, leaving tails intact. Reserve the prawns. Place the prawn shells and heads in a saucepan with the water and simmer for 20 minutes to make stock. Discard shells and reserve stock.

TO COOK the laksa, heat the oil in a large saucepan. Add the laksa paste; stir until aromatic and oil separates from the paste. Add some prawn stock and thin coconut milk, stirring constantly until boiling. Do not stop stirring, or coconut milk may curdle. Slowly add the thick coconut milk, reserved prawns and fish pieces (if using). If using tofu and mushrooms, add them now. Leave simmering until ready to serve and dilute as necessary with remaining prawn stock or water. To serve, place the warm noodles in a bowl. Top with hot laksa and add garnishes to taste.

SERVES 4

LAKSA PASTE To a food processor or blender, add 6 dried chillies, 2 stalks finely sliced lemon grass, 1 tablespoon chopped galangal or laos powder, 1 teaspoon ground turmeric and 2 tablespoons shrimp paste. Blend to form a smooth paste, adding some water or coconut milk if necessary.

LEFT: Laksa Lemak, a Malaysian soup
rich with coconut milk and redolent
with fresh spices

FISH GRILLED OVER VINE CUTTINGS

I first had fish grilled this way in the Hunter Valley, the famous wine district of New South Wales. The vines are pruned each autumn and the cuttings are dried and saved for burning, the smoke of which gives a delicious and distinctive flavour. If vine cuttings are not available, use small twigs of sweet-smelling wood or fennel.

INGREDIENTS

1–1.5 kg (2–3 lb) snapper, coral trout, salmon or jewfish, cleaned
salt and freshly ground black pepper
2–3 sprigs fresh tarragon
1–2 tablespoons olive oil
vine cuttings or other small, sweet wood twigs
lemon wedges, to serve

A FISH-shaped basket with short legs is ideal for grilling fish over dried vine cuttings; you can also use a folding wire-hinged barbecue grid. Build the fire in a small barbecue grill. Season the fish cavity and skin with salt and pepper. Place the tarragon sprigs in the cavity and skewer the fish closed. Place in the basket. Brush generously with the olive oil. Vine cuttings burn fast, so have plenty on hand to add to the fire as needed. Lay the fire in an oval shape a little longer than the fish grill, light, and, when very hot, place fish grill slightly to the leeward side of the fire.

GRILL the fish, flipping the basket to turn the fish as it browns and cooks, basting with more oil as it cooks. Keep the fire hot. The fish is done when it flakes with a fork. This will take about 15 minutes if the fish is turned carefully and the fire is kept burning furiously. Place the fish on a platter and garnish with lemon wedges. Serve immediately.

FENNEL

Fennel is a perennial herb found growing wild along many river banks and country roads. You will recognise the long, thin stems with yellow flowers and feathery leaves.
Pick bundles, long stems and flowers, tie with string and hang to dry under cover. You can also buy dried fennel in many delicatessens and kitchen shops.

FISH GRILLED OVER WILD FENNEL

Fish is first grilled on the barbecue or hibachi on barbecue beads or wood as in the above recipe, allow about 2–5 minutes on each side. Long stalks of dried fennel are put under the fish—they catch alight and give their lovely aromatic flavour to the fish during the last 5 minutes of cooking. Fennel burns fast, so you will need plenty of dried stalks on hand.

PRAWNS WRAPPED IN SPINACH LEAVES

A lovely light Thai salad of prawns (shrimp). Each diner can use the spinach leaves to wrap up their serving of prawns. Lettuce leaves can be used in place of the spinach.

INGREDIENTS

1 bunch spinach leaves

1 lime, peeled and cut into small
cubes

2.5 cm (1 in.) piece of ginger, peeled
and finely chopped

2 red bird's eye chillies, finely sliced

4 tablespoons peanuts, roasted and
coarsely ground

4 tablespoons shredded coconut,
roasted

¼ stalk tender lemon grass, finely
sliced

500 g (1 lb) cooked prawns
(shrimp), peeled and deveined

Thai Shrimp Dressing (below)

WASH the spinach leaves, snip off stalks and spin dry. Arrange little pile of spinach leaves on 4 serving plates. Combine the remaining ingredients in a large bowl and gently fold to mix. Divide the prawn mixture and pile onto the spinach leaves or beside them. Lastly, spoon over the Thai Shrimp Dressing.

SERVES 4

COCONUT

The coconut used in this recipe may be fresh whole coconut or packaged. To grate fresh coconut, cut coconut to open and prise out the flesh, the pieces can then be grated or shredded. Roast under a hot grill (broiler) or in a dry frying pan or skillet.

THAI SHRIMP DRESSING

Anyone who has eaten in Thai restaurants knows the importance of dressings and dips.

INGREDIENTS

1 tablespoon sliced galangal, roasted
lightly in a dry frying pan

2 teaspoons dried shrimp

4 tablespoons shredded coconut,
roasted

1 teaspoons shrimp paste, roasted

4 tablespoons fish sauce (nam pla)

1 cup (250 mL/8 fl oz) water

ADD the galangal, dried shrimp, coconut and shrimp paste to a food processor or blender. Blend to a fine paste. Combine with the fish sauce and water in a small saucepan and simmer for 10 minutes until the sauce has reduced by half. Strain and cool before using.

NOTE Galangal is similar in appearance to fresh ginger and adds a wonderful flavour to many Thai dishes. It is available fresh and also in a dried form under the Indonesian name of *laos* which is soaked before using.

SALMON AND ASPARAGUS ON ROCKET

This is a fresh light way of serving salmon. Take care not to have the grill too hot or it will dry the salmon. The leeks should be done at the last moment.

INGREDIENTS

2 bunches fresh asparagus

1 bunch rocket (arugula)

4 salmon cutlets or fillets

light olive oil, for frying

salt and freshly ground black pepper

½ leek, cut into julienne

SAUCE

½ cup (125 mL/4 fl oz) dry white wine

2 tablespoons fresh (single, light) cream

125 g (4 oz) butter, cubed

juice of 1 lime

TRIM the asparagus and thinly peel half the stalk at the lower end. Wash the rocket and drain. Preheat the grill (broiler) or ribbed grill. Brush the salmon on both sides with olive oil and sprinkle with salt and pepper to taste. Arrange the salmon on a grilling rack and place about 10 cm (4 in.) from the source of the heat. Grill for about 8–10 minutes, turning halfway through cooking. The fish is done when the centre bone comes away easily from the flesh. If using a ribbed grill, allow to get hot over a high heat. Brush the salmon with olive oil and cook for about 6 minutes, turning once. Remove and keep warm on a heated platter covered with foil while cooking the asparagus.

MEANWHILE, in a small saucepan, heat enough oil to deep-fry the leeks. Fry the leeks over a moderate heat until golden and crisp. Drain on absorbent paper towels.

TO MAKE the sauce, reduce the white wine by two-thirds in a small saucepan. Add the cream and reduce further. Lastly, add the butter, a small amount at a time, stirring. Add the lime juice. Keep warm.

DROP the asparagus into simmering salted water and cook gently for about 3 minutes, drain and refresh under cold water. Arrange the rocket on 4 serving plates. Divide the asparagus among the plates, placing on top of the rocket. Top with the salmon cutlets and spoon over the sauce. Sprinkle with the deep-fried leeks and serve.

SERVES 4

RIGHT: Salmon and Asparagus on Rocket, a wonderful and easy-to-prepare warm salad

FISH WITH HERB CRUST AND BASIL HOLLANDAISE

*This recipe uses fresh fish fillets cooked in a herbed breadcrumb crust.
The crisp, golden crust keeps the flesh succulent and a wonderfully rich,
sharp but unctuous sauce is the perfect marriage.*

INGREDIENTS

1 cup (60 g/2 oz) fresh breadcrumbs

*2 tablespoons chopped fresh
herbs such as parsley, basil,
chervil, chives*

1 egg

2 tablespoons milk

*4 × 200 g (7 oz) white fish fillets,
such as orange roughy, boned and
skinned*

salt and freshly ground pepper

30 g (1 oz) butter

1 tablespoon olive oil

Basil Hollandaise (below)

COMBINE the breadcrumbs and herbs. In a separate bowl, beat the egg lightly and add the milk. Whisk to combine. Season the fish fillets lightly with salt and pepper, and dip into the egg mixture. Coat with the breadcrumb mixture. Melt the butter and oil in a heavy frying pan and cook the fish on each side for just 2–3 minutes. Serve the crusty fish on 4 heated dinner plates with a little of the Basil Hollandaise. Extra hollandaise can be offered in a small bowl.

SERVES 4

BASIL HOLLANDAISE

*This lovely sauce is good with poached, grilled or fried fish dishes. It is
also delicious with chicken fillets, either grilled or pan-fried.*

INGREDIENTS

2 egg yolks

2 teaspoons cold water

125 g (4 oz) butter

pinch of cayenne pepper

*¼ cup fresh basil leaves, finely
chopped*

*1 tablespoon fresh (single, light)
cream*

1 tablespoon lemon juice

IN A bowl, combine the egg yolk with the water. Whisk over a pan of gently simmering water until fluffy. Slowly add the butter, whisking all the time as you would when adding oil to mayonnaise, until thickened. Add the cayenne pepper, basil, cream and, lastly, the lemon juice.

MAKES ½ CUP

GRILLED TIGER PRAWNS

*Large tiger prawns (shrimp), like all shellfish, are best eaten
from their shells. Do not overcook.*

INGREDIENTS

*12 large raw tiger prawns (shrimp)
  or scampi*

3 tablespoons extra virgin olive oil

*few sprigs of fresh oregano and
  thyme, chopped*

*2 tablespoons chopped flat-leaf
  (Italian) parsley*

2 cloves garlic, finely chopped

½ red chilli, seeded and chopped

freshly ground black pepper

lemon wedges, to serve

SPLIT the prawns or scampi lengthwise through the centre, devein
and arrange, cut side up, on a large shallow dish. Combine the oil with
the chopped herbs, garlic and chilli. Drizzle the flavoured oil over the
shellfish and season with freshly ground pepper. The shellfish can be
prepared ahead up to this stage.

PREHEAT the grill (broiler) and arrange the shellfish, cut side up,
on the grilling pan. Cook until the flesh has turned white, about
3–5 minutes. Remove from the heat and arrange on a large serving
platter with the lemon wedges. Have a bowl on the table for the
discarded shells, and finger bowls with a slice of lemon. To eat the
shellfish, use a fork to pull out the tail meat. Serve with crusty bread
and, if liked, a bowl of mayonnaise (page 25) mixed with a little sweet
chilli sauce.

SERVES 4

FISH STEAKS WITH
BALSAMIC VINEGAR

*Grilled fish responds well to the flavours of good olive oil and balsamic
vinegar, which enhance it with a wonderful aromatic fragrance.*

INGREDIENTS

*4 snapper or jewfish steaks, about
  2.5 cm (1 in.) thick, or fillets*

1 tablespoon olive oil

1 teaspoon balsamic vinegar

1 spring onion (scallion), chopped

dash of Tabasco sauce

freshly ground black pepper

PREHEAT the grill (broiler), including a flat tray underneath. Line
the heated tray with oiled foil; lay fish on the foil. If grilling fillets, have
the skin side up and score the skin in one or two places. Mix together
the remaining ingredients and use to brush fish steaks. Grill fish about
5 cm (2 in) from the heat, basting until the fish flakes easily, about
2–4 minutes on each side (fillets don't need to be turned). Serve with
lemon wedges, crusty bread or steamed potatoes, and a salad.

SERVES 4

SAFFRON RICE WITH SEAFOOD

In this splendid Spanish dish, use seafoods of your choice, or small chicken joints which should be half-cooked with the onions before adding the rice.

INGREDIENTS

good pinch of Spanish saffron
 threads
3 cups (750 mL/24 fl oz) light fish
 or chicken stock
2 tablespoons olive oil
2 medium onions, chopped
1½ cups (250 g/8 oz) long-grain rice,
 rinsed
250 g (8 oz) green prawns (shrimp),
 shelled and deveined
12 mussels or baby clams (pippies),
 well washed
small bunch of fresh coriander
 (Chinese parsley)

HEAT the saffron in the stock and leave to infuse. Heat the olive oil in a frying pan, paella or flattish casserole, and gently cook the onions until soft and golden. Add the rice and cook, stirring until well coated with oil. Add the hot stock, stirring until the mixture comes to the boil, reduce the heat and simmer gently for 10 minutes. Add the prawns pressing gently into the rice. Continue to cook for 5 minutes. Add the prepared mussels or clams, which should open with the heat. If you have a lid, part-cover the rice. When the rice is tender (about 18–20 minutes in all), remove from the heat and gently fluff up the rice with a fork. Sprinkle coriander sprigs over the top and serve.

SERVES 6

FISH STOCK

This stock is used in many fish sauces and soups. It can be frozen or will keep well in the refrigerator for up to a week.

INGREDIENTS

2 kg (4 lb) bones, heads (without
 gills) or trimmings of any white,
 non-oily fish
5 cups (1.25 litres/2 imp. pints) cold
 water
1 cup (250 mL/8 fl oz) white wine
 or the juice of 1 lemon plus
 enough water to make 1 cup
1 teaspoon white peppercorns
bouquet garni

PLACE all the ingredients in a saucepan and bring to the boil. Skim the surface and simmer very gently for 20 minutes. Strain through a fine sieve or cheesecloth. Store in an airtight container.

MAKES 6 CUPS

NOTE Fish stock must be simmered, never boiled. Do not throw away crab, lobster or prawn (shrimp) heads. Put them in the freezer in plastic (polythene) bags; they will keep there and be ready to toss in the stockpot when you need some fish stock.

RIGHT: Saffron Rice with Seafood, a Spanish dish celebrating the sublime seasoning, saffron

SALMON TARTARE WITH GINGER MAYONNAISE

Atlantic salmon or the large salmon trout are such a treat and this is a simple way to enjoy them as a first course. The fish is not cooked, but rather marinated for a short while.

INGREDIENTS

375 g (12 oz) Atlantic salmon or sea trout, skin removed

1 small red salad onion or spring onion (scallion), finely diced

salt and freshly ground black pepper

2 tablespoons vodka or gin

ginger mayonnaise (add 1 teaspoon grated fresh ginger to homemade mayonnaise; page 25)

FINELY dice the salmon or trout flesh. Put into a bowl with the onion and vodka or gin. Season with salt and a good grinding of pepper. Mix lightly, cover and refrigerate for 30 minutes or longer. To serve, use 6 entrée plates. Place a couple of spoonfuls of salmon or trout tartare on each plate with a spoonful of the ginger mayonnaise just before serving. Serve with slices of pumpernickel or rye bread.

SERVES 6

TUNA TARTARE Cut tender raw pink tuna into tiny cubes and toss with finely diced salad onion, capers and chilli. Serve on rounds of fried bread or pumpernickel as a refreshing and simply made cocktail canapé.

TUNA CARPACCIO WITH HERBS

Most good delicatessens serve preserved lemons. They are salty but add a piquant flavour. They are one of the main flavourings in Moroccan tagines, and salads.

INGREDIENTS

400 g (13 oz) sashimi-quality tuna

extra virgin olive oil

2 teaspoons finely diced preserved lemon

few leaves of fresh basil, finely shredded

1 teaspoon fresh oregano leaves

juice of 1 lemon

freshly ground black pepper

freshly snipped chives, to garnish

USING a very sharp knife, cut the tuna into very thin slices. To make the slices even thinner, arrange on sheets of lightly oiled plastic wrap, cover with additional sheets of wrap and gently roll with a rolling pin; be careful not to tear the flesh. Roll up the sheets loosely and chill the tuna for at least an hour or until ready to use. Preheat a grill (broiler). Arrange the tuna slices on 4 dinner plates and drizzle each with a little olive oil. Scatter with the preserved lemon, basil and oregano. Sprinkle with the lemon juice. Season with a good grinding of pepper. Briefly warm the tuna under the grill for about 30 seconds on the plates, two at a time. Remove and sprinkle with the snipped chives. Serve with a green salad in separate bowls alongside.

SERVES 4

STEAMED SAFFRON MUSSELS

INGREDIENTS

2 kg (4 lb) mussels

3 spring onions (scallions), chopped

1 cup (250 mL/8 fl oz) white wine

½ cup (125 mL/4 fl oz) water

6 thin slices leek, white part only,
   or 6 thin slices onion

1 small carrot, sliced

½ bay leaf

4 sprigs fresh parsley

½ cup (125 mL/4 fl oz) fresh (single,
   light) cream

good pinch of saffron threads

2 tablespoons lemon juice

salt and freshly ground pepper

freshly chopped parsley (extra)

SCRUB the mussels, removing any dark beard around the edges, and wash thoroughly in several changes of water. Discard any that do not shut when tapped. Soak in cold water for 1 hour, then drain. Place the mussels in a wide pan with the shallots, wine, water, leek or onion, carrot, bay leaf and parsley sprigs. Cover and cook over a high heat for 5 minutes, shaking the pan now and then. Remove the mussels, as soon as they open, discarding half of each shell. Discard any mussels that do not open. Strain the cooking liquid, wipe the pan and return the liquid to the pan. Bring to the boil, then add the cream and saffron, and reduce over a high heat for 1–2 minutes. Add the lemon juice and season with salt and pepper. Return the mussels to the pan and heat through. Serve in 4 shallow bowls, strewn with chopped parsley, with some crusty bread.

SERVES 4

THAI SEAFOOD AND BASIL

INGREDIENTS

1 kg (2 lb) mixed seafood such as
   squid, green prawns (shrimp)
   (shelled and deveined), firm white
   fish fillets (cubed) and scallops
   (brown parts removed)

2 tablespoons vegetable oil, plus
   1 teaspoon extra

2 medium onions, cut into eight
   segments

3 cloves garlic, peeled and thinly
   sliced

½ cup fresh basil leaves

1 fresh red bird's eye chilli, halved,
   seeds removed and sliced

fish sauce (nam pla), to taste

CUT the squid into large squares, then score into tiny cubes—do not cut right through—to make it tender when cooked.

HEAT the 2 tablespoons oil in a wok or heavy frying pan, and stir-fry the squid for a few minutes. Remove, then add the prawns and cook until turned pink. Remove and, lastly, add the fish and scallops, and cook until whitened and just tender. Set all aside together.

ADD the extra oil to the wok and stir-fry the onions and garlic over a brisk heat until aromatic and golden. Stir in the basil leaves, then return the seafood to the wok or pan. Add the chillies and stir-fry for a further minute, then sprinkle with the fish sauce to taste. Serve hot with Steamed Aromatic Rice (page 104).

SERVES 4–6

STIR-FRIED TURBOT WITH SHIITAKE MUSHROOMS

A welcome addition at my local fish market is the large variety of flat fish now available. It may be grilled or fried whole, or given a new twist and stir-fried. Other firm, white fish fillets may also be cooked this way.

INGREDIENTS

750 g (1½ lb) fish fillets such as turbot, brill, sole or flounder

3 tablespoons light sesame oil

1 clove garlic, finely chopped

1 teaspoon freshly grated ginger

1 red bird's eye chilli, seeded and chopped

12 shiitake mushrooms, stems trimmed and halved if large

4 golden shallots, thinly sliced

4 spring onions (scallions), cut into 5 cm (2 in.) lengths

1 tablespoon soy sauce

sprigs of fresh coriander (Chinese parsley), to garnish

YOU can ask the fishmonger to fillet the whole fish for you. Skin the fillets and cut into bite-sized chunks. Heat the sesame oil in a wok or large frying pan, add the fish pieces, garlic, ginger and chilli, tossing very gently. Remove and set aside.

REHEAT the pan with a little extra oil and add the mushrooms, shallots and spring onions. Toss for 2 minutes or until the vegetables are crisp and tender. Add the soy sauce and return the fish to the wok or pan, and stir gently. Garnish with the coriander sprigs and serve with Steamed Aromatic Rice (page 117).

SERVES 4

NOTE Flat fish include: sand flounder, yellowbelly flounder, lemon sole, Dover and New Zealand sole, brill and turbot. All these fish have fine, delicate flesh with clean flavours. Turbot and brill are the more robust, and will stir-fry brilliantly.

SESAME OIL

The light-coloured oil is found in most health food stores and is made with untoasted sesame seeds; it is used with other oil for frying foods. The amber-coloured oil, which is made from toasted sesame seeds, is used sparingly and at the end of cooking for flavouring. Store all oils in a cool, dark place.

RIGHT: Stir-Fried Turbot with Shiitake Mushrooms, made with tender loving care—it is bliss

SWEET TREATS

NOTHING turns a house into a home like the warm aroma of freshly baked bread and cakes. There is nothing like a proper pudding to remind us of our childhood, to make our eyes light up, to make us feel loved. When there is a celebration to be had, there is a fitting cake or dessert—gâteau Saint-Honoré, the wonderful French birthday cake, English Christmas cake rich with fruits, a yule log for Christmas eve, fig pies for figgy Sunday (Palm Sunday), simnel cake for Easter or Mother's Day.

GOOD things from the oven cheer us up whenever they appear. It is well established that a good orange cake is always the first to go at a school or church fête. The little kourambiedes which I make as gift offerings, which are reputed to be the best biscuits in the world. People are known to travel halfway across our city for a true almond friandise. Suzanne's fig tart and chocolate dacquoise are just two of the speciality dishes that woo her friends to dine at her table. A good recipe is all you need to create them in your own home. They are included in this chapter.

SOMETIMES all one wants for dessert is a piece of perfectly ripe fresh fruit. When such fruits are in season, they are also plentiful. The passionate cook knows how to turn these fruits into the most delectable sweet things. Pears with caramel and the intriguing flavour of cardamom. Figs appear in port wine, and wonderful combinations like rhubarb and strawberries appear under a crumbly crust to update a great cobbler. Highland mist appears with gently poached fruit such as tamarillos.

IF YOU have never made bread or baked a cake, if you don't know the joy baking the perfect offering or gift in your own kitchen, now is the time to start. There is a spiritual solace in baking and making desserts; it is one of the pleasantest ways of enjoying the good life. Join the club!

DESSERTS AND FRUITS

I particularly enjoy fruit desserts, freshly prepared—grilled figs, baked pears, a lightly cooked compôte of fruits in wine. I can't resist creamy desserts—a lovely bavarois with a fresh raspberry coulis, or a gratin of fresh fruits under a caramelised cream. A warm, old-fashioned cobbler or steamed pudding, or an English fool, is irresistible. With so many delicious desserts, it's no wonder that we all have more than one or two favourites.

CARAMELISED CARDAMOM PEARS

Pears are perfect poached, baked, grilled (broiled) or sautéed, or simply wash and eat. Choose firm but ripe pears for this superb dessert.

INGREDIENTS

60 g (2 oz) unsalted butter, plus
  2 teaspoons extra
½ cup (90 g/3 oz) soft brown sugar
1 teaspoon ground cardamom
½ cup (125 mL/4 fl oz) water
6 ripe pears, peeled, halved and
  cored
2 tablespoons dark rum
mascarpone, to serve

PREHEAT the oven to 220°C (425°F). In a saucepan, melt the butter over a moderate heat and stir in the sugar, cardamom and water. Cook until the sugar is dissolved. Place the pears in a buttered, shallow ovenproof baking dish. Spoon over the caramel mixture and toss to coat; dot with the extra butter. Bake in the oven, uncovered, for 20 minutes, basting the pears several times with the pan juices.

TRANSFER the pears with a slotted spoon onto 4 dessert plates. Stir the rum into the syrup until well combined. Scoop a spoonful of mascarpone onto each plate and spoon syrup over the pears.

SERVES 4

BEURRE BOSC

An elegant pear with greenish-brown skin that warms to a dark cinnamon brown when ripe, the beurre bosc has a delicate texture and flavour. Often selected for the cheese tray, this ideal dessert pear is perfect in this recipe. Bartlett and Packham pears are also suitable.

GRATIN OF MIXED BERRIES

INGREDIENTS

1 punnet strawberries, halved

1 punnet raspberries

1 punnet blueberries

1 egg yolk per person

*1 tablespoon caster (superfine) sugar
per person*

*½ cup (125 mL/4 fl oz) crisp, dry
Champagne or dry white wine*

icing (confectioners') sugar, to serve

PREHEAT the grill (broiler) to very hot. Using a large heat-resistant serving pan or 4 heatproof serving plates, arrange the mixed berries on the bottom of the dish or plates. Whisk the egg yolks and sugar together in a bowl over a pan of simmering water. Whisk in the Champagne; continue to beat until the mixture is light and fluffy, and slightly thickened. Remove from the heat and continue to whisk until cooled slightly.

SPOON the sauce over the fruit, sprinkle lightly with icing sugar and place under the very hot grill for a few moments until lightly coloured.

SERVES 4–6

VINTNER'S COMPOTE

*Winemakers know the joys of both drinking wine and using it in the food
they prepare. The compôte of dried fruit will keep refrigerated for more than
a week; the grapes are best added just before serving.*

INGREDIENTS

*6 each dried pears, nectarines and
apricots*

1 cup (250 mL/8 fl oz) water

*½ cup (125 g/4 oz) white granulated
sugar*

½ vanilla bean

1 stick cinnamon

*1 cup (250 mL/8 fl oz) Chardonnay
or Riesling*

*2 strips of orange rind, cut into fine
needles*

1 cup (250 g/8 oz) black grapes

1 cup (250 g/8 oz) white grapes

PUT the dried fruits in a saucepan and cover with the water. Bring slowly to the boil, reduce the heat and gently simmer for about 15 minutes. Drain and turn into a bowl. Add the sugar, vanilla and cinnamon stick to the fruit liquid. Bring to the boil, simmer for 5 minutes, add the wine and simmer for a further 2–3 minutes. Pour the syrup over the poached fruit and chill. Meanwhile, seed the grapes, if necessary, using a large darning needle. If the skins are thick, peel. Add with orange rind to the chilled fruit. Serve with pouring cream, ice cream or sour cream to which has been added a tablespoon of soft brown sugar.

SERVES 6

LEFT: Gratin of Mixed Berries—fruit under a light sauce is gratinéed to serve just warm. Sliced figs or peaches may be added when they are in season

RHUBARB STRAWBERRY COBBLER

Strawberries partner with rhubarb like magic, whether in a jam, a tart, a fool, a pie or a cobbler.

INGREDIENTS

1 bunch rhubarb, washed, trimmed
  and cut into 3 cm (1¼ in.) pieces

1 cup (250 g/8 oz) white granulated
  sugar, plus extra

2 tablespoons cornflour (cornstarch)

4 tablespoons water

2 punnets strawberries, hulled and
  halved

1 teaspoon grated orange rind

1½ cups (185 g/6 oz) self-raising
  flour

large pinch of salt

60 g (2 oz) unsalted butter

1 egg, lightly beaten

3 tablespoons milk

freshly whipped cream, to serve

PREHEAT the oven to 200°C (400°F). Toss the rhubarb with the sugar and cornflour, and turn into a buttered 7-cup (1.75 litre/3 imp. pint) baking dish that is at least 6 cm (2½ in.) deep. Add the water.

COVER the dish with foil and bake in the oven for 20–30 minutes, or until tender. Remove from the oven and add the strawberries and orange rind. Toss well together. Meanwhile, sift the flour into a bowl with the salt and rub in the butter using your fingers. Lightly beat the egg and milk together. Mix into the dry ingredients until just combined. Drop the dough in large spoonfuls over the fruit and sprinkle with extra sugar. Return to the oven and bake for a further 15–20 minutes, until the top is golden brown. Serve warm with whipped cream or ice cream.

SERVES 6–8

MANGO AND LIME CARPACCIO

A fabulous combination of two tropical fruits—a perfect summer dessert!

INGREDIENTS

½ cup (125 mL/4 fl oz) water

rind of 1 lime, cut into julienne

⅓ cup (90 g/3 oz) white granulated
  sugar

juice of 2 limes

3 mangoes, peeled and thinly sliced

IN A small saucepan bring the water to the boil, then drop in the lime rind. Add the sugar, stir until dissolved, then allow the syrup to boil for 3 minutes. Lastly, stir in the lime juice. Arrange the mango slices decoratively on 6 serving plates. When the syrup is cool enough, pour it over the mango slices. Leave to macerate for an hour or so before serving.

SERVES 6

GRILLED FIGS IN PORT

Ripe luscious figs are one of the delights of summer. Serve warm with a port wine syrup and creamy mascarpone—something wonderful to enjoy.

INGREDIENTS

½ cup (125 mL/4 fl oz) port wine

½ cup (125 mL/4 fl oz) water

3 tablespoons soft brown sugar

1 vanilla bean

1 stick cinnamon

8–12 large fresh figs

1 cup (250 mL/8 fl oz) mascarpone

4–6 mint sprigs (optional)

dessert biscuits, to serve

PREHEAT the grill (broiler) to hot. Place the port, water, brown sugar, vanilla bean and cinnamon stick in a saucepan. Bring slowly to the boil, stirring. Simmer, partially covered, for 10 minutes or until reduced by half. Meanwhile, cut the figs into quarters halfway down from the stem and open out slightly like a flower. Place the figs cut side up in a flameproof dish. Spoon some of the port mixture over each fig. Place under the grill to glaze for a few minutes.

CAREFULLY arrange the figs on dessert plates. Set a large scoop of the mascarpone alongside the figs and drizzle over the juices in the dish. Garnish, if liked, with mint sprigs and a dessert biscuit.

SERVES 4–6

TIRAMISU

There are many versions of this popular desssert—this is my first choice.

INGREDIENTS

6 large egg yolks

3 tablespoons caster (superfine) sugar

3 tablespoons Marsala or *brandy*

1¾ cups (435 mL/14 fl oz) mascarpone

1 cup (250 mL/8 fl oz) thickened (double, heavy) cream

3 tablespoons Tia Maria or coffee-flavoured liqueur

½ cup (125 mL/4 fl oz) strong espresso coffee, cooled

16–20 sponge fingers

2 tablespoons cocoa powder, sifted

PLACE the egg yolks in a bowl and beat until thick and creamy. Place the bowl over a saucepan of simmering water and keep beating, gradually adding the sugar, and then the Marsala or brandy. Keep beating until the mixture is thick and fluffy. Remove from the heat and continue beating until cooled.

IN A mixing bowl, beat the mascarpone until smooth. In another bowl, whip the cream until stiff and fold in the mascarpone. Fold the cream and mascarpone mixture into the chilled Marsala mixture. Combine the liqueur and coffee. Line a glass baking dish with half the sponge fingers. Brush with the coffee mixture. Spoon half the mascarpone mixture over the biscuits. Top with the remaining biscuits to form another layer, brush with the coffee mixture and smooth the rest of the mascarpone mixture on top. Cover with plastic wrap and chill for several hours before serving. To serve, cut into squares and dust with sifted cocoa.

SERVES 8

HIGHLAND MIST

*Excellent use is made of good-quality whisky in the highlands of
Scotland; the better the whisky, the better the results.
I use my best highland malt.*

INGREDIENTS

18–20 coconut macaroons

*2–3 tablespoons fresh (single, light)
cream*

4 tablespoons whisky

*1 cup (250 mL/8 fl oz) double (light
whipping) cream, whipped with
½ teaspoon vanilla essence
(extract)*

*strawberries, sliced, or other small
berry or poached fruit*

WITH a rolling pin, crush the macaroons then place in a bowl. Add
the cream and whisky, and stir the mixture to a paste. Spread a layer of
the mixture in a small crystal or glass bowl, or use individual glass
dishes—wine glasses are ideal. Cover with a layer of vanilla whipped
cream. Repeat the layers until all the macaroon mixture is used and
finish with a layer of whipped cream. Chill the mist and serve with
fresh sliced strawberries or fresh poached tamarillos, or any choice of
soft or poached fruits in season and a crisp biscuit.

SERVES 6

POACHED TAMARILLOS

*The tamarillo is native to South America—a glossy, plum-red or golden
yellow fruit the size of an egg, with juicy, slightly acid flesh that may
be used raw in salads or poached.*

INGREDIENTS

1½ cups (375 mL/12 fl oz) water

½ cup (125g/4 oz) granulated sugar

*½ vanilla bean or 1 teaspoon vanilla
essence (extract)*

12 fresh tamarillos

IN A saucepan, bring the water, sugar and vanilla slowly to the boil.
When the sugar is dissolved add the tamarillos, reduce the heat and
poach the fruit for 5–6 minutes. Remove the fruit and boil the syrup to
reduce by about half. Peel the fruit, put in a bowl, cover with syrup
and refrigerate until required. Serve whole or halved with cream,
custard or Highland Mist (above). For a sweeter taste to the Highland
Mist, sprinkle over demerara or soft brown sugar.

SERVES 6

POACHED PEARS Peel 6 firm pears, halving if large, and poach
as above.

POACHED PEACHES, NECTARINES AND PLUMS
Wash, halving fruit if large, and poach as above.

POACHED APPLES Peel and quarter apples, and poach
as above.

RIGHT: Highland Mist may be served
with berry fruits or as in the picture
with Poached Tamarillos

STICKY DATE PUDDING

These are the lightest, best little puddings you could ever imagine. I cook them in individual pudding moulds, but you could make one large pudding and steam for 1 hour, or bake into two loaf pans and cut into slices to serve. Serve with Caramel Sauce or thick cream or, better still, both.

INGREDIENTS

2 cups (375 g/12 oz) pitted dates

1¼ cups (310 mL/10 fl oz) water

1½ teaspoons bicarbonate of soda (baking soda)

½ cup (125 g/4 oz) unsalted butter, softened

¾ cup (185 g/6 oz) caster (superfine) sugar

3 large eggs

1 teaspoon vanilla essence (extract)

2 cups (250 g/8 oz) self-raising flour

1 teaspoon ground ginger

Caramel Sauce (below)

PREHEAT the oven to 180°C (350°F). Butter and flour eight ½-cup (125 mL/4 fl oz) ramekins. In a small saucepan, cover the dates with the water and bring slowly to the boil. Stir in the bicarbonate of soda and set aside. In the bowl of an electric mixer, beat the butter and sugar until the mixture is light and fluffy. Add the eggs, one at a time, beating well after each addition, then add the vanilla. Sift the flour with the ginger, and fold into the butter mixture. Mash the date mixture with a fork (this can also be done in a food processor). Lightly fold into the batter.

DIVIDE the mixture among the ramekins and bake on a baking sheet in the middle of the oven for 15–20 minutes, or until a skewer comes out clean. Let the puddings cool in the ramekins for 10 minutes, then run a sharp knife around the edge of each ramekin and transfer the puddings, bottom sides down, to dessert plates. Serve warm with the Caramel Sauce.

SERVES 8

CARAMEL SAUCE

This luscious sauce is good served warm with ice cream and is wonderful with steamed puddings.

INGREDIENTS

1 cup (250 mL/8 fl oz) fresh (single, light) cream

½ cup (125 g/4 oz) unsalted butter

½ cup (100 g/3½ oz) soft brown sugar

1 tablespoon golden syrup or *maple syrup*

IN A saucepan, combine the cream, butter, brown sugar and syrup. Bring the mixture to the boil, stirring, and boil the sauce for 2–3 minutes, or until it thickens slightly.

VANILLA BAVAROIS WITH FRESH RASPBERRY COULIS

Bavarois or Bavarian cream is a timeless classic. These days, it is moulded individually and accompanied by a little fruit coulis. I like to use a fresh vanilla bean to flavour the milk and scrape out some of the seeds to add a fleck to the bavarois.

INGREDIENTS

1½ cups (375 mL/12 fl oz) milk

1 vanilla bean or 2 teaspoons
   vanilla essence (extract)

4 egg yolks

¾ cup (185 g/6 oz) caster (superfine)
   sugar

pinch of salt

1 tablespoon gelatine, softened in
   3 tablespoons cold water

1½ cups (375 mL/12 fl oz) (light
   whipping) cream

Raspberry Coulis (below)

a few fresh raspberries or
   strawberries, to decorate

SCALD the milk with the vanilla bean (if using), cover and cool. Beat egg yolks with sugar and salt until thick and lemon coloured. Place in a heavy pan with the milk and stir over a low heat until the mixture coats the back of a spoon. Remove the vanilla bean, cool slightly and scrape some of the seeds into the hot custard mixture. Add the softened gelatine, stir until dissolved and then add the vanilla essence if not using the vanilla bean.

COOL, then chill until the mixture is beginning to set, stirring frequently. Whip the cream until soft peaks form and fold through the custard. Pour into 6 individual dariole moulds which have been lightly oiled and chill for several hours until firm. Unmould carefully onto serving plates and surround each with a little raspberry coulis, decorating with the fresh berries.

SERVES 6

FRESH RASPBERRY COULIS

INGREDIENTS

1 cup (250 g/ 8 oz) raspberries or
   hulled strawberries

1 tablespoon redcurrant jelly

½ cup (90 g/3 oz) caster (superfine)
   sugar

juice of ½ lemon

GENTLY heat the raspberries or strawberries until just lukewarm. Add the redcurrant jelly, caster sugar and lemon juice, lightly mashing the fruit. Mash to a pulp, then push through a sieve.

CHOCOLATE DACQUOISE

This lovely meringue dessert with a crisp outside and a softer, slightly fudgy centre is a classic. The nuts should be freshly blanched for a fuller flavour.

INGREDIENTS

5 egg whites

1 cup (225 g/7 oz) caster (superfine) sugar

½ cup (90 g/3 oz) blanched almonds, roughly chopped

pinch of cream of tartar

1¼ cups (300 mL/10 fl oz) (light whipping) cream

125 g (4 oz) dark (semi-sweet) chocolate, melted

icing (confectioners') sugar

grated chocolate or Chocolate Caraque (below), to decorate

PREHEAT the oven to 140°C (275°F). Make sure the bowl you select for beating the egg whites is perfectly clean and dry. Whisk the egg whites in a large bowl using a balloon whisk or an electric mixer until very stiff. Add 5 teaspoons caster sugar and whisk for 1 minute. Fold in the remaining caster sugar, almonds and cream of tartar until just mixed. Spread the mixture out with a knife into two rounds on baking trays (sheets) lined with baking parchment. (By first marking the paper with circles the size of dinner plates, you will get the rounds the same size.) Bake in the oven for 1–1½ hours, or even longer; when cooked, the underside should have no sticky patches. Cool on wire racks. Once cooled, sandwich with the whipped cream, which has been mixed with the cooled melted chocolate. Dust with the icing sugar and decorate with grated chocolate or Chocolate Caraque.

SERVES 8–10

CHOCOLATE CARAQUE

Gently melt 100 g (3½ oz) dark (semi-sweet) chocolate onto a plate over a pan of hot water. Do not allow the plate to get too hot and work the chocolate with a palette knife as it melts. Spread it thinly on a marble slab. When just on point of setting, curl it off with a thin knife—the chocolate will form long scrolls or flakes after a little practice. Place on greaseproof (wax) paper and chill in the refrigerator until ready to use.

RIGHT: Chocolate Dacquoise is one of the great classics, a dessert for celebrations

CHAPTER 11

HOME BAKING

There's something about home-baked bread and cakes that goes straight to the heart. A good recipe is esssential, although previous generations of cooks relied on a sure eye and an experienced hand —until you have both, don't experiment; follow a recipe and you'll soon be turning out wonderful treats.

FLAT PIZZA BREAD

Sometimes called focaccia *or* schiacciata, *this flat bread can simply be sprinkled with sea salt and olive oil as I've done here, or sprinkled with halved black olives, thinly sliced onions or sprigs of herbs.*

INGREDIENTS

*15 g fresh yeast or 1 envelope
  (7 g) dry yeast
2–2½ cups (500–625 mL/
  16–20 fl oz) warm water
4 cups (500 g/16 oz) plain
  (all-purpose) flour
3 tablespoons virgin olive oil
coarse sea salt*

DISSOLVE the yeast in ½ cup (125 mL/4 fl oz) warm water and allow to stand for 10 minutes. Place the flour on a work surface and make a well in the centre. Pour the dissolved yeast into the flour with the remaining water and 1 tablespoon oil to make a soft dough. Knead until very smooth and elastic, for 5–10 minutes. Form the dough into a ball. Brush the inside of a large bowl with a little olive oil and add the ball of dough. Cover with plastic wrap then a cloth, and leave to stand in a warm place until the dough has doubled in bulk.

KNEAD the dough again very lightly. Roll out on a lightly floured baking tray into a large circle, oval or rectangle about 1 cm (½ in.) thick. Cover and leave to rise again for 20 minutes. Preheat the oven to 230°C (450°F). Brush or drizzle the top of the dough with the remaining olive oil and sprinkle with the salt. Bake in the oven until golden brown, about 20–25 minutes.

SERVES 6–8

OLIVE BREAD

This is a great bread and it makes wonderful sandwiches—try a soft cheeese and some prosciutto, or a tasty cheese with celery.

INGREDIENTS

30 g (1 oz) fresh yeast or
  2½ teaspoons dry yeast
4 cups (500 g/16 oz) plain (all-purpose) or baker's white flour
2 teaspoons white granulated sugar
warm water, plus ⅓ cup (90 mL/ 3 fl oz) extra
¾ cup (125 g/4 oz) pitted black olives
salt and freshly ground black pepper
4 tablespoons olive oil
maize meal or white flour, for dusting

BLEND the yeast with a little of the flour and a little of the sugar in a small amount of the warm water, and leave in a warm place for 10–15 minutes. Set aside 8–10 olives and roughly chop the rest. Mix together the remaining flour, sugar, yeast mixture, chopped olives and salt and pepper to taste in a bowl. Make a well in the centre and add the extra warm water and the olive oil. Mix to form a dough and knead for about 10 minutes, until the dough is smooth and elastic. Place in a greased bowl and sprinkle with a few drops of water. Cover bowl with plastic wrap and leave in a warm place for 1½–2 hours.

KNEAD the dough again, then shape it into a 20 cm (8 in.) round, place on a greased and floured baking sheet, sprinkle with a little flour and cover with a cloth. Leave for a further 1½–2 hours, until the dough has doubled in size. Preheat the oven to 200°C (400°F), then press the whole olives into the top of the dough and make a cross in the top of the loaf with a sharp knife. Bake for 20 minutes, then reduce the oven temperature to 180°C (350°F). Bake for a further 25–30 minutes, or until cooked through, well risen and golden. Allow to cool on a wire rack and sprinkle with a little maize meal or white flour.

MAKES 1 LOAF

OLIVE CHEESE BREAD Make as for Olive Bread, but add 30 g (1 oz) grated tasty cheese such as cheddar and 2 tablespoons grated Parmesan cheese, at the same time as the chopped olives.

CUTTING AND SLASHING

Cutting or slashing the loaf gives certain loaves their characteristic appearance and helps to give them a kind of secondary crust for varying colour. It takes a little practice, but for loaf bread the cuts should be made after 10 minutes of proving in their tins. Crusty loaves that are baked directly on the baking sheet are cut just before being put in the oven, or they will spread too much.

ORANGE WALNUT BAR

This is a great personal favourite and one I like to make often. It may be frosted, but I prefer it plain.

INGREDIENTS

125 g (4 oz) unsalted butter

¾ cup (185 g/6 oz) caster (superfine) sugar

grated rind of 1 orange

grated rind of 1 lemon

2 eggs

1½ cups (185 g/6 oz) self-raising flour, sifted

½ cup (60 g/2 oz) chopped walnuts

½ cup (125 mL/4 fl oz) orange juice

3 tablespoons milk

2 teaspoons white granulated sugar

PREHEAT the oven to 180°C (350°F). Grease a 4–5 cup (1–1.25 litre/1¾–2 imp. pint) loaf pan well with butter and line the base of the pan with baking parchment. Using an electric mixer, cream the butter, caster sugar and grated orange and lemon rind until light and fluffy. Add the eggs, one at a time, beating well after each addition. Gently fold through the sifted flour; stir in the walnuts, orange juice and milk.

POUR into the prepared pan and sprinkle thickly with the sugar. Bake in the oven for about 50 minutes. Test with a fine skewer before removing from the oven. Stand for a few minutes, then cool on a wire rack.

SERVES 8–10

GALETTE AUX NOISETTES

This French cake—flattish as a galette should be—is one of the more delicious nut cakes.

INGREDIENTS

200 g (7 oz) butter

¾ cup (185 g/6 oz) caster (superfine) sugar

3 large eggs

2 cups (200 g/7 oz) ground almonds (almond meal)

2 cups (200 g/7 oz) ground hazelnuts

½ cup (60 g/2 oz) plain (all-purpose) flour

200 g (7 oz) unsalted butter

icing (confectioners') sugar

PREHEAT the oven to 230°C (450°F). Butter a 25 cm (10 in.) straight-edged flan ring or cake pan, preferably with a loose bottom. Line the base with baking parchment. Cream the butter and beat in the sugar until light and fluffy. Add the eggs, one at a time, beating well after each addition. Stir in the nuts and flour, mixing gently but firmly. Turn into prepared pan and spread out roughly at first to fit the pan, then cover with plastic wrap and smooth the dough with the palm of your hand.

BAKE in the oven for 12–15 minutes. Unmould and cool. Dust with sifted icing sugar. As this cake is rather rich, cut into fairly thin wedges.

SERVES 6–8

LEFT: Orange Walnut Bar, a favourite with tea or coffee, or serve with cream as a dessert

PRUNE ARMAGNAC GINGERBREAD

A rich-tasting and very special moist gingerbread studded with prunes.

INGREDIENTS

1 cup (185 g/6 oz) chopped pitted prunes

½ cup (125 mL/4 fl oz) Armagnac or other brandy

1 tablespoon grated fresh ginger

3 cups (375 g/12 oz) plain (all-purpose) flour

2 teaspoons bicarbonate of soda (baking soda)

2 teaspoons ground cinnamon

1 teaspoon ground ginger

1 teaspoon ground cloves

½ teaspoon salt

125 g (4 oz) unsalted butter, at room temperature

1½ cups (250 g/8 oz) firmly packed light brown sugar

1 cup (250 mL/8 fl oz) treacle

½ cup (125 mL/4 fl oz) strong brewed coffee or water

4 large eggs, lightly beaten

icing (confectioners') sugar, for dusting

PREHEAT the oven to 180°C (350°F). Butter a 25 cm (10 in.) springform pan and line the base with baking parchment. In a small saucepan, cook the prunes, Armagnac and grated ginger over a medium heat, stirring frequently, until almost all the liquid is evaporated. Remove the pan from the heat.

INTO a bowl, sift the flour, bicarbonate of soda, cinnamon, ginger, cloves and salt. In the bowl of an electric mixer, cream the butter. Add the brown sugar, beating until the mixture is light and fluffy. Add the treacle in a stream, beating until well combined. Beat in the coffee or water, flour mixture, and eggs until the batter is just combined. Stir the prune mixture into the batter. Turn the mixture into the prepared pan.

BAKE in the centre of the oven for 1 hour 20 minutes, or until a toothpick comes out clean, and cool on a rack for 1 hour. It may be necessary to cover the cake with brown paper if it is browning too much before it is cooked through. (The gingerbread will fall slightly in centre.) Dust with icing sugar to serve. Serve cooled or warm, with or without whipped fresh cream.

SERVES 8–10

ARMAGNAC

Armagnac is a French brandy produced in the Department of Gers, southeast of Bordeaux, and named after the village of Armagnac. It has a drier, harsher taste than Cognac and for this reason is preferred by some connoisseurs. It adds distinction to this bread, although brandy is also good—the finer the Armagnac or brandy is, the better the flavour.

GLAZED LEMON AND BUTTERMILK CAKE

*This cake has a marvellous refreshing fresh lemon tang. Buttermilk
is a wonderful addition to cakes, muffins and scones (biscuits),
giving a light moistness to their texture.*

INGREDIENTS

250 g (8 oz) unsalted butter, at
  room temperature
1½ cups (350 g/11 oz) caster
  (superfine) sugar
3 eggs
3 cups (375 g/12 oz) plain
  (all-purpose) flour
½ teaspoon bicarbonate of soda
  (baking soda)
½ teaspoon salt
1 cup (250 mL/8 fl oz) buttermilk
2 tablespoons fresh lemon juice
2 tablespoons lemon rind
Lemon Glaze (below)

PREHEAT the oven to 160°C (325°F). Grease a 25 cm (10 in.) ring
tin (tube pan) with butter. Using an electric mixer, cream the butter
until softened. Beat in the sugar, beating until light and fluffy. Beat in
the eggs, one at a time. Sift the flour, bicarbonate of soda and salt, and
fold into the creamed mixture alternately with the buttermilk and
lemon juice and rind. When combined, turn the mixture into the
prepared pan. Bake in the centre of the oven for 1 hour, or until a fine
skewer inserted comes out clean and the cake pulls away slightly from
the edges. Leave the cake to cool in the pan, set on a rack for
10 minutes, before carefully turning out. Spread with the Lemon Glaze
while still hot.

SERVES 6–8

LEMON GLAZE

This buttery glaze melts into the hot cake, imparting its fresh tang.

INGREDIENTS

60 g (2 oz) unsalted butter, softened
1½ cups (250 g/8 oz) icing
  (confectioner's) sugar, sifted
2 tablespoons grated lemon rind
3 tablespoons lemon juice

CREAM the butter and sugar until light and fluffy. Gradually mix in
the lemon rind and juice, and spread over the hot cake.

ENOUGH FOR 1 CAKE

ALMOND FRIANDISES

In French pastry terms, a friandise is a small dainty cake often served with afternoon tea or coffee. They keep fresh for days. As these cakes are larger than a mouthful, they may be cut in two or three for dainty eating.

INGREDIENTS

185 g (6 oz) butter

½ cup (90 g/3 oz) blanched almonds

1 cup (100 g/3½ oz) ground almonds (almond meal)

1⅔ cups (300 g/10 oz) icing (confectioners') sugar, sifted

⅓ cup (75 g/2½ oz) plus 1 tablespoon plain (all-purpose) flour, sifted

5 egg whites

10–12 oval friandise moulds (½ cup size) or 24 small patty pans (muffin pans)

GREASE the moulds or patty pans well with butter. Preheat the oven to 230°C (450°F). Put the butter in a small saucepan; cook gently until it is pale gold. Pour into a small jug and set aside.

PUT the blanched almonds in the bowl of a food processor fitted with a metal blade and process the almonds until roughly chopped. Add the ground almonds, sifted icing sugar and sifted flour, and process until mixed. Add the egg whites and the warm butter, pouring the butter in carefully to hold back any of the browned solids that will sink to the bottom of the jug. Mix together well.

SPOON the mixture into the prepared moulds or patty pans, about half filling each mould. Place on a baking sheet and bake in the oven for 5 minutes. Reduce the heat to 200°C (400°F) and bake for a further 12–15 minutes. The patty pans will take 8–10 minutes. Turn off the heat and leave the cakes in the oven for 5 minutes. Remove from the oven and turn out onto a wire rack.

MAKES 11–12

COCONUT DROPS

Dainty sweet morsels are welcome on the tea tray, with coffee or dessert.

INGREDIENTS

1½ cups (185 g/6 oz) self-raising flour

pinch of salt

1 cup (225 g/7 oz) white sugar

1 egg, lightly beaten

1 teaspoon vanilla essence (extract)

few drops of almond essence (extract)

125 g (4 oz) butter, melted

1⅓ cups (125 g/4 oz) desiccated (dried grated) coconut

PREHEAT the oven to 180°C (350°F). Grease 2 baking sheets or line with baking parchment. Sift the flour and salt into a bowl and stir in the sugar. Add the remaining ingredients, except the coconut, and combine. Form the mixture into small balls about the size of a marble and roll in the coconut. Arrange on the prepared baking sheets, spacing well apart. Bake in the oven for 15 minutes or until golden. Remove and cool on a wire rack. Store in an airtight container.

MAKES ABOUT 30

RIGHT: Almond Friandises—these little French cakes are a delectable treat, perfect with afternoon tea or after-dinner coffee

PARISIENNE ALMOND TART

A delectable French almond tart which will keep for several days. A fine dusting of icing (confectioners') sugar is its traditional finish.

INGREDIENTS

1 quantity rich shortcrust pastry
(below)
2 egg whites
1 cup (250 g/8 oz) white granulated
sugar
2 cups (225 g/7 oz) flaked or
slivered blanched almonds
¼ teaspoon ground cinnamon
1 teaspoon vanilla essence (extract)
icing (confectioners') sugar, for
dusting (optional)

PREHEAT the oven to 190°C (375°F). Make the pastry, wrap and chill for a least 1 hour. Roll out on a floured board to fit a flan ring at least 25 cm (10 in.) in diameter or 10 cm × 25 cm (5 in. × 10 in.). Trim away excess pastry and prick the base lightly with a fork. Line the shell with baking parchment and half fill with rice or dried beans. Chill for a further 15 minutes.

BAKE in the oven for 15 minutes. Remove the paper and rice, and bake the shell for a further 5 minutes until pale golden. To make the filling, combine the egg whites, sugar, almonds, cinnamon and vanilla in a saucepan. Heat, stirring all the time, until the mixture is hot, but do not boil. Pour the filling into the pastry shell and bake in the oven for 20–25 minutes until golden and firm. Dust with icing sugar (if using) and cut the tart into wedges or squares while still warm.

SERVES 8–10

RICH SHORTCRUST PASTRY

Pastry should be made an hour before required then chilled for a crisp fine crust.

INGREDIENTS

1½ cups (185 g/6 oz) plain
(all-purpose) flour
pinch of salt
90 g (3 oz) chilled butter, diced
1 tablespoon caster (superfine) sugar
1 egg yolk
2 teaspoons iced water
squeeze of lemon juice

SIFT the flour and salt together in a bowl. Rub in the butter until the mixture resembles coarse breadcrumbs, then toss in the sugar. Mix the egg yolk, water and lemon juice together, and stir into the flour quickly with a knife to form a dough. Shape into a ball, wrap in plastic film and chill for 20 minutes before rolling and shaping. Chill again before baking.

MAKES 1 PASTRY SHELL

CHOCOLATE ALMOND WAFERS

*These crisp almond wafers are very simple to make and are great
with desserts or ice cream.*

INGREDIENTS

⅔ cup (75 g/2½ oz) slivered almonds

½ cup (125 g/4 oz) caster (superfine)
  sugar

2 egg whites

3 teaspoons unsalted butter, melted

4 tablespoons plain (all-purpose)
  flour

1 tablespoon cocoa powder

pinch of salt

PREHEAT the oven to 160°C (325°F). Roast the slivered almonds
in a single layer on a baking sheet until lightly golden, about
20 minutes. Cool and set aside. In a bowl, whisk the sugar, egg whites
and melted butter together. Stir in the flour sifted with the cocoa
powder and salt until smooth and well combined. Stir in the roasted
almonds. Cover the mixture and stand at room temperature for
20 minutes. Trace 2 × 23 cm (9 in.) circles on a piece of baking
parchment on a baking sheet. Bake in the oven for 20–25 minutes, or
until cooked through and crisp. Allow to cool for 3–5 minutes only
before cutting into thin wedges. Store in an airtight container.

MAKES ABOUT 32 WEDGES

KOURAMBIEDES

*These little morsels pierced with a clove and coated with icing
sugar are the ultimate Greek shortbread.*

INGREDIENTS

250 g (8 oz) unsalted butter

4 tablespoons caster (superfine)
  sugar

1 egg yolk

3 cups (375 g/12 oz) plain
  (all-purpose) flour, sifted

½ cup (60 g/2 oz) finely chopped
  almonds

60 whole cloves

icing (confectioners' sugar), sifted,
  for dusting

PREHEAT the oven to 150°C (300°F). Grease 2 baking sheets.
Cream the butter and gradually beat in the caster sugar until light and
fluffy. Add the egg yolk and beat well. Stir the sifted flour into the
creamed mixture alternately with the almonds. Knead the mixture
lightly and form into a ball. Roll small pieces of dough into balls the
size of a small walnut and press a whole clove into the centre of each,
or shape into crescents. Place on the prepared sheets and bake in the
oven for 25–30 minutes, or until lightly coloured. Do not brown.
While still warm, sprinkle with the sifted icing sugar. When cool, place
in an airtight container.

MAKES ABOUT 60

INDEX